D1461678

STUDENT UNIT GUIDE

NEW EDITION

AQA(B) A2 Psychology Unit 4

Approaches, Debates and Methods in Psychology

Regina Teahan

Series editor: Julie McLoughlin

PHILIP ALLAN

Philip Allan Updates, an imprint of Hodder Education, an Hachette UK company, Market Place, Deddington, Oxfordshire OX15 0SE

Orders

Bookpoint Ltd, 130 Milton Park, Abingdon, Oxfordshire OX14 4SB
tel: 01235 827827
fax: 01235 400401
e-mail: education@bookpoint.co.uk
Lines are open 9.00 a.m.–5.00 p.m., Monday to Saturday, with a 24-hour message answering service. You can also order through the Philip Allan Updates website: www.philipallan.co.uk

ISBN 978-1-4441-6230-1
2011001141
First printed 2012
Impression number 5 4 3 2 1
Year 2016 2015 2014 2013 2012

Cover photo: Andreas Karelias/Fotolia

Typeset by Integra, India

Printed in Italy

Hachette UK's policy is to use papers that are natural, renewable and recyclable products and made from wood grown in sustainable forests. The logging and manufacturing processes are expected to conform to the environmental regulations of the country of origin.

P2030

Contents

Content guidance

Questions & Answers

Getting the most from this book

Examiner tips
Advice from the examiner on key points in the text to help you learn and recall unit content, avoid pitfalls, and polish your exam technique in order to boost your grade.

Knowledge check
Rapid-fire questions throughout the Content guidance section to check your understanding.

Knowledge check answers

1 Turn to the back of the book for the Knowledge check answers.

Summary

Summaries

● Each core topic is rounded off by a bullet-list summary for quick-check reference of what you need to know.

Questions & Answers

Exam-style questions

Examiner comments on the questions
Tips on what you need to do to gain full marks, indicated by the icon e.

Sample student answers
Practise the questions, then look at the student answers that follow each set of questions.

Questions & Answers

Question 2 **Approaches in psychology (II)**

(a) Outline two methodological criticisms of the person-centred approach of Rogers and Maslow. (4 marks)

e This question is assessing your knowledge of 'how science works' by asking you to take a critical look at how humanistic psychologists go about investigating individual subjective conscious experience. You must take care not to get sidetracked into an outline of how they investigate such experience, but go beyond that and consider the problems with their methods. Also, be careful not to go into problems with their actual theories, although the way one investigates a phenomenon can, of course, have implications for the theory under study. To answer this question you need to identify and outline criticisms around issues such as reliability, validity, falsifiability, sampling, generalisability and objectivity.

(b) Use an example of behaviour to explain what cognitive psychologists mean by mediational processes. (4 marks)

e This part is essentially asking you to do two things. First of all, you should state clearly what the term 'mediational processes' means. This term is in the specification under social learning theory but applies equally to the cognitive approach. Any term that appears on the specification can be tested in this manner. The more difficult part is the second requirement of the question and involves conveying the meaning of the term through an example.

(c) Outline and compare the cognitive and behaviourist approaches in psychology. (12 marks)

e This section requires an extended answer and you will be assessed on the quality of your written communication as well as the psychological content. In this question, the bulk of the marks are for discussion, so focus on comparing. One third of the marks are reserved for knowledge and understanding, which means you should include an outline of each approach. It is a good idea to use specialist terminology, as this will also gain marks if relevant. When comparing, you can of course point out differences between the two approaches as well as similarities. Think about theoretical and methodological comparisons (theories and research methods). Remember that in these 12-mark questions, you need to show the examiner that you have a really good overview of psychology as a whole, so it is a good idea to link into topic areas, debates or other approaches to broaden your discussion.

Student A

(a) One methodological criticism of the person-centred approach is that it is not scientific a. Another is that the approach is culture bound b and cannot be easily applied to different societies like people in the third world c. This is because it was only tested d on people like Lincoln and Eleanor Roosevelt c.

e 1/4 marks awarded. a The student has correctly identified one way, which gains a mark; this is the reference to the approach not being scientific. There is no elaboration of this point, which would have gained another mark if accurate. b The second way — mentioning that the approach is 'culture bound' (presumably concepts and ideas) — is not a methodological criticism. c The last sentence is getting closer to answering the question, but if the use of the term 'tested'

64

AQA(B) A2 Psychology

Examiner commentary on sample student answers
Find out how many marks each answer would be awarded in the exam and then read the examiner comments (preceded by the icon e) following each student answer. Annotations that link back to points made in the student answers show exactly how and where marks are gained or lost.

About this book

This is a guide to Unit 4 of the AQA(B) A2 Psychology specification. It is intended as a revision aid rather than as a textbook. Its purpose is to summarise the content, to explain how the content will be assessed, to look at the type of questions to expect and to consider specimen answers.

There are three main topic areas in Unit 4 and you have to answer questions on each of these topics in your examination. You must answer one Option from a choice of two on Approaches in Psychology, plus the compulsory questions on Debates in Psychology and the compulsory questions on Methods in Psychology.

For each of these topic areas, this guide will cover the following:
- The specification content, including exactly what you need to know and learn. The coverage of the content is minimal, as you should already have learned the detailed content in your studies. The focus is on key terms and concepts, theories and studies and evaluation points. The content here is not the only appropriate material; textbooks will cover the topics in various ways and probably give much more detail and alternative studies.
- Six example questions, two for each of the topic areas. These questions will be in the style of AQA(B) A2 questions and similar to those that you might expect to see on real examination papers. To accompany each question there is analysis of how the question should be tackled and what the examiners are looking for in an answer.
- For each question there are *two* sample answers, A and B. One answer is probably what would be typical of a grade C/D performance and the other is a high scoring answer that might be typical of those awarded a grade A in the examination. Each answer is followed by a detailed commentary about the marks that have been awarded, drawing attention to any errors or points that are especially creditworthy. There are also suggestions as to how the answers might be improved or elaborated upon to get extra marks. If you read these sample answers and comments carefully you will learn a lot about what you need to do to present a really effective answer in the examination.

How to use this guide

First check your class notes and revision notes against the content presented here to make sure that you have all the right material for your revision. Then look at a sample question to see how the exam is structured and what is required. Have a go at the question yourself then review the sample answers and comments to see where marks can be gained and lost. The sample answers are not intended as model answers but as tools to help you understand what makes a good answer. Finally, you should review your own answer in the light of what you have read and consider how it might be improved.

Content guidance

In this section, content guidance is offered on the topic areas of approaches, debates and methods in psychology. Each topic begins with a summary of the AQA Specification B requirements for Unit 4. This is followed by a brief account of the theories and concepts that make up the unit content.

Knowledge of appropriate theories and concepts is essential for the A2 examination. It is also important to be able to assess their value, and this is done here with regular 'Evaluation' features.

Names and publication dates have been given when referring to research studies. The full details for these studies are normally available in textbooks, should you wish to research the topic further.

Approaches in psychology

Summary specification content

The assumptions and applications of the following approaches: biological; behaviourist; social learning theory; cognitive; psychodynamic and humanistic. The strengths and limitations of each approach.

You are expected to know the key features/**assumptions** of each approach. All the approaches have already been covered at AS but you may find it useful to revise their content. At A2 you also need to consider how the approaches have been **applied** to topic areas in psychology, including their practical applications, and to demonstrate that you have a broad and critical appreciation of each approach. Therefore you need to consider both theoretical and methodological issues when discussing their **strengths** and **limitations.**

Biological approach

Specification content

The role of the central and autonomic nervous system in behaviour and the genetic basis of behaviour.

The biological approach looks to biology as a means of describing and explaining psychological functioning. It focuses on two internal components of human beings: their physiological make-up and genetic inheritance.

Knowledge check 1

What name is given to the chemical substance produced by an endocrine gland?

Examiner tip

Avoid simply stating that 'you cannot generalise (extrapolate) from animals to humans' when discussing the biological approach. Be prepared to justify your answer. You could discuss specific examples of research, or broader issues such as the position taken by humanistic psychologists.

The basic **assumptions/features** of the biological approach are as follows:

- Physiological processes affect behaviour, mood and cognition. Psychology should therefore investigate the nervous system (particularly the brain), brain chemicals and the endocrine system.
- Genes affect behaviour and influence individual psychological differences between people. Evolutionary psychology considers genetic influences in common behaviours.
- According to Darwin's theory of evolution there is behavioural continuity between species. The study of animals can be of relevance in attempting to understand human behaviour.
- The biological approach draws on concepts from the hard sciences and research tends to be highly scientific in nature. The most common methods include laboratory experiments and observations, including the use of objective brain recording and scanning techniques.

Role of the central and autonomic nervous system in behaviour

Central nervous system (CNS)

The central nervous system (brain and spinal cord) plays an essential role in co-ordinating behaviour. Psychologists are mainly concerned with the activities of the higher centres of the brain which control complex voluntary behaviour. It is here that processes such as thinking, remembering, problem solving and language occur. Brain chemicals such as dopamine pass information between nerve cells and are thus also implicated in behaviour.

Autonomic nervous system (ANS)

The CNS is connected to the rest of the body by the peripheral nervous system (PNS). One aspect of the PNS is the autonomic nervous system (ANS), which controls the self-regulating activities of internal organs and glands, e.g. heartbeat. The ANS is sub-divided into two parts: the sympathetic and parasympathetic systems. The sympathetic system serves an arousing function and mobilises the body for action in times of stress or threat. The parasympathetic system serves to restore or conserve energy resources after the threat has passed. The sympathetic division is involved in emotions such as fear and anger.

The ANS also governs the endocrine system, which has a more long-term effect on behaviour through the release of hormones, e.g. testosterone is linked with increased levels of aggression.

Genetic basis of behaviour

The basic units of heredity are called genes. Genes function in pairs and the recombination of genes from parents to offspring provides the basis for genetic variability. There is evidence from twin (monozygotic (MZ) and dizygotic (DZ)) adoption and family studies to suggest that genes are implicated in certain behaviours such as autism and schizophrenia. However, genes only determine the potential for a characteristic (genotype). The observable characteristics of an individual (phenotype) depend on the *interaction* of genetic and environmental factors.

> **Examiner tip**
> You need to be able to demonstrate your knowledge and understanding of how scientists investigate the biological basis of behaviour.

> **Examiner tip**
> Think of a topic you have studied that considers biological explanations of behaviour such as autism or anxiety disorders. Make notes on how you might use the evidence on brain activity in a discussion on the role of the CNS in behaviour.

> **Knowledge check 2**
> Identify three physiological changes that occur when the sympathetic nervous system prepares the body for action in times of threat.

> **Examiner tip**
> Do not include aspects of physiological psychology such as the central and peripheral nervous systems in answer to questions on the genetic basis of behaviour.

> **Knowledge check 3**
> Distinguish between monozygotic and dizygotic twins.

Strengths of the biological approach

- It gives an appreciation of the role of physiology and genes in behaviour, cognition and mood. It shows how human behaviour might be constrained by its evolutionary past. Research provides insights into biochemical and genetic influences on mental and emotional disorders.
- Valuable evidence has accumulated about the biological basis of behaviour. This has resulted in useful practical applications, e.g. drugs for mental disorders.
- This approach is particularly scientific. Its subject matter is materialistic and its methods are objective.
- It provides strong counter-arguments to the nurture side of the 'nature–nurture' debate.

Limitations of the biological approach

- The physiological system is complex and therefore the biological approach is not sufficiently advanced to offer complete explanations of behaviour.
- There are endless environmental influences so it is difficult to predict behaviour and explain it in purely biological terms (biological reductionism). Influences interact so it is difficult to draw specific conclusions about one factor, e.g. genetic links with schizophrenia, without taking into account other factors such as social, cultural and family influences.
- The approach seems to suggest that mind and brain are the same but has not explained how these interact. The mind/consciousness is difficult to study objectively.
- Biological causes of behaviour result in the problem of determinism, absolving people from responsibility in their behaviour.

Application of the biological approach (examples)

Topic area	Application
Gender development	**Testosterone** is a possible biological cause of gender differences. It is associated with increased aggression. **Evolutionary psychology:** aggressiveness in males is an adaptive behaviour for hunting/competition.
Memory	The hippocampus (part of the limbic system in the **forebrain**) plays an important role in memory. Damage to this area results in an inability to form new memories.
Schizophrenia and mood disorders	Role of **chemicals** (e.g. dopamine and serotonin); **genes**; **brain** abnormalities (e.g. enlarged ventricles — schizophrenia). Use of anti-psychotic **drugs** to treat schizophrenia.
Stress	Close interaction between behaviour and physiological changes; the role of the **autonomic nervous system**.
Autism	**Genetic** explanations, abnormalities in the **frontal lobes** (planning and control), **limbic system** (emotional regulation), **brain stem** and **cerebellum** (motor coordination).

After studying this topic, you should be able to:

- describe the assumptions (features) of the biological approach
- understand that the biological approach is concerned with both how our genetic inheritance and physiology (the structure, function and processes of the nervous system) affect how we think, feel and behave
- describe the role of the central nervous system and autonomic nervous system in behaviour
- outline and discuss examples of the genetic basis of behaviour
- explain how scientists investigate the biological basis of behaviour
- evaluate the biological approach, providing supporting evidence for your argument
- discuss applications of the biological approach

Behaviourist approach

Specification content

Key concepts including stimulus, response and reinforcement. Types of reinforcement. Classical and operant conditioning as applied to human behaviour.

The behaviourist approach focuses on overt and measurable behaviour. It takes an extreme nurture approach and looks to theories of learning to explain psychological functioning. It focuses on two theories of learning: **classical** and **operant** conditioning.

The basic **assumptions/features** of the behaviourist approach are as follows:
- Psychology should adopt an objective and scientific approach.
- Observable behaviour only should be studied, not minds. Mental processes are impossible to observe, cannot be part of the scientific subject matter of psychology and are not required to explain behaviour.
- Most behaviour is learned from the environment after birth (the child at birth is like a *tabula rasa* or blank slate). Psychology should therefore investigate the laws of learning.
- Learning can be understood in terms of conditioning principles and involves an association between a **stimulus** and a **response**. Even complex behaviour can be reduced to simple stimulus–response (S–R) associations.
- The laws of learning are universal and apply to both animals and humans.

Key concepts

Stimulus   Anything, internal or external, that brings about a response.

Response   Any reaction in the presence of a stimulus.

Reinforcement   The process by which a response is strengthened.

Examiner tip
When explaining the learning of behaviour, avoid using words such as 'thinks', 'knows' 'remembers'. These are mental processes that cannot be observed. Instead of writing 'the animal thinks that he will receive food if he presses the lever', write 'the animal associates lever pressing with food'.

Examiner tip
Remember! No conscious or mental activity is involved in conditioning.

Knowledge check 5
How did behaviourists operationalise the 'strengthening of a response'?

Examiner tip

To remember the terms, think of 'unconditioned as 'natural' or 'unlearned', and 'conditioned' as acquired because of certain 'conditions'. It is natural to salivate in the presence of food but not when you hear a bell. This response occurs because of certain conditions: when the bell rings, food follows. The bell ringing becomes associated with food.

Examiner tip

In the exam, make sure you use behaviourist terminology such as conditioned stimulus, unconditioned response, reinforcement. The use of psychological terminology is taken into account when marking your answer.

Knowledge check 6

In the example of advertising, identify the UCS and the CS.

Types of reinforcement

Positive — response is followed by something pleasant.

Negative — response is followed by the removal of something unpleasant.

Classical conditioning as applied to human behaviour

In classical conditioning (learning through association), a neutral stimulus becomes associated with a natural stimulus–response (reflex) connection and a new behaviour link may be formed. This was demonstrated by Pavlov when studying salivation in dogs. The whole process can be shown as follows:

Stages involved in Pavlovian conditioning

Stage 1	Food (UCS) elicits salivation (UCR)
Stage 2	Food (UCS) + bell (CS) elicits salivation (UCR)
Stage 3	Bell (CS) elicits salivation (CR)

UCS = unconditioned stimulus; CS = conditioned stimulus;
UCR = unconditioned response; CR = conditioned response.

Stimuli similar to the CS, e.g. a church bell or clinking keys could trigger the same conditioned response (generalisation). The effects of conditioning can extend into new learning situations.

The theory of classical conditioning has been applied to behaviour in two ways:

To explain behaviour

Classical conditioning can explain behaviour that is linked to emotions, e.g. the acquisition of phobias. A person may learn to fear a previously neutral stimulus, e.g. a spider, if it is connected to a frightening event. A scream produces fear so if someone screams in the presence of a spider, an association is quickly made between the two stimuli because of their temporal contiguity (occurrence at the same time).

Advertising campaigns often apply the principles of classical conditioning. Advertisers use pictures associated with strong emotional UCSs that elicit strong positive reactions, e.g. romantic meetings paired with alcohol.

To treat behaviour

Classical conditioning techniques (behaviour therapy) have been used to treat phobias and addictions. In treating phobias, the aim of the treatment is to extinguish the link between the CS and the CR. This can be done in three ways: systematic desensitisation, implosion and flooding.

In treating addictions, aversion therapy is used to create a phobia of the object of addiction. For example, in treating alcoholism this can be done by repeatedly giving a vomit-inducing drug with alcohol.

Operant conditioning as applied to human behaviour

In operant conditioning (learning through association between response and consequence) the person or organism 'operates' in its environment, resulting in consequences. Positive and negative reinforcement increase the probability of a behaviour being repeated, whereas punishment decreases this probability. If a child says 'thank you' in the presence of adults and is praised, then this behaviour is likely to occur again. Conversely if the child is caught swearing and punished, then this behaviour is less likely to occur again (at least in the presence of adults).

Operant conditioning has also been applied to the treatment of behaviour (behaviour modification). Maladaptive (undesired) behaviour is seen simply as the consequence of faulty learning so can be treated through behaviour shaping.

Examples include social skills training, which involves teaching appropriate social skills by using rewards, and token economy systems used in institutions, whereby tokens are given as secondary reinforcement for good behaviour.

Application of the behaviourist approach (examples)

Topic area	Application
Anxiety disorders	Phobias are learned through **classical conditioning** and maintained through **negative reinforcement. Operant conditioning** explains how compulsive acts are learned through reinforcement by fear reduction. Treatment, e.g. systematic desensitisation and flooding.
Autism	Treatment, e.g. behaviour modification and aversion therapy.
Schizophrenia and mood disorders	Behavioural treatment for schizophrenia involving **tokens** as **secondary reinforcers**. Behavioural explanations of depression consider the role of **reinforcement** and **punishment**.
Stress management	Behavioural approaches to stress management include **biofeedback** and **systematic desensitisation**.
Substance abuse	**Aversion therapy** is used in the treatment of substance abuse.

Strengths of the behaviourist approach

- Behaviourism is very scientific. Theories are testable and supported by rigorous experimental research. Behaviourism has left a lasting legacy; its scientific approach influencing all areas of psychology.
- Behaviourist explanations can be applied to the real world to explain everyday behaviour such as gambling and has produced many practical applications.
- It provides strong counter-arguments to the nature side of the 'nature–nurture' debate.

Examiner tip

Be careful not to confuse negative reinforcement with punishment. The aim of negative reinforcement is to draw out the correct response. Punishment tries to suppress the wrong response. It may help to think as follows: punishment is like saying 'stop it'; negative reinforcement is like saying 'do it again'.

Examiner tip

'Reward' has a very specific meaning and must not be used to mean reinforcement. Reinforcement strengthens a response and is sometimes the removal of something unpleasant, such as pain (negative reinforcement) and not the giving of something pleasant. A reward may not always strengthen a response: for example, praise could be embarrassing.

Knowledge check 7

Identify two key features of behaviour shaping.

Examiner tip

Take care to elaborate when you evaluate. For example, if you make the point that many forms of learning cannot be satisfactorily explained by classical and operant conditioning, tell the examiner why conditioning fails to explain the behaviour. Do not simply provide a list of examples of behaviour.

What is meant by 'secondary reinforcement'?

Limitations of the behaviourist approach

- Behaviourism ignores important mental processes involved in learning and innate predispositions to produce certain responses.
- Many forms of learning cannot be satisfactorily explained by classical and operant conditioning, e.g. insight learning or observational learning.
- There are philosophical concerns: behaviourism is mechanistic, deterministic and thus unable to explain the human capacity for free will. It is also reductionist (reducing complex human behaviour to a few simple principles of learning).
- Much data has been obtained from species such as rats, dogs and pigeons but the relevance of these findings to human behaviour is dubious.

Summary

After studying this topic, you should be able to:
- describe the assumptions (features) of the behaviourist approach
- understand that the behaviourist approach is concerned only with observable behaviour
- know and use key behaviourist terminology
- describe the acquisition of behaviour through both classical and operant conditioning
- explain how behaviourists investigate the acquisition of behaviour
- evaluate the behaviourist approach, providing supporting evidence for your argument
- discuss applications of the behaviourist approach

Social learning theory

Specification content

The role of mediational processes in learning, motivation and performance of behaviour. Observational learning and the role of vicarious reinforcement.

Social learning theory forms a bridge between traditional behaviourism and the cognitive approach. The behaviourist approach explains all behaviour by stimulus, response and reinforcement, whereas social learning theory also considers social and cognitive processes in learning. It is concerned with human rather than animal behaviour and proposes that learning can occur simply by observing others. Social learning theory sees people as active manipulators of their own environment rather than passive receivers of experiences.

The basic assumptions or features of social learning theory are as follows:
- Learning occurs through the observation of role models.
- **Observational learning** can take place without any reinforcement — simply observing the model is sufficient for learning to occur.
- Reinforcement is important for the **performance** or **imitation** (**modelling**) of the learned behaviour. Reinforcement may be direct or indirect (**vicarious reinforcement**).
- Observational learning involves cognitive processes such as memory. These processes occur between stimulus and response and are known as **mediational processes**.
- Much human behaviour is learned in interpersonal situations.

Distinguish between direct reinforcement and indirect (vicarious) reinforcement.

It is important to understand that, according to social learning theory (SLT), while reinforcement may be important for the performance of learned behaviour, it is not essential to learning itself. Learning can happen without reinforcement. This is a crucial distinction between SLT and the behaviourist approach.

Cognitive factors that determine whether imitation takes place are:

- **Attention.** Models that are not relevant to the observer attract little attention. The most influential models are those who are similar, liked, admired and respected, have a high status and also ones who are seen to be reinforced.
- **Retention.** Information acquired from observing the model is stored in memory. These memories, including whether they were reinforced or punished, influence future behaviour.
- **Judgement.** Appraisal of one's own capacity for motor reproduction of the observed behaviour.
- **Motivation.** Reinforcement (direct and vicarious), punishment, expectations of success or failure and confidence in one's own ability all determine whether a behaviour is to be performed.

Study

Bandura et al. (1963) studied the role of imitation in learning aggressive behaviour. They used two groups of children. The experimental group saw an adult in a room full of toys being violent to an inflatable Bobo doll, while the control group saw the adult playing non-violently. Each child was then left alone in the room with the toys and observed on film. Without any direct encouragement, the experimental group performed significantly more aggressive acts on the doll than the control group. They also used many of the same movements they had just seen.

Evaluation

- The researchers did not measure long-term effects and the study has been criticised for being artificial. However, the findings are consistent with other experimental studies which have demonstrated that children are more likely to hurt other children after viewing violent behaviour. The study reveals that observation, cognitive factors and imitation are important in learning. Direct personal experience and reinforcement are not required for learning to occur, though Bandura agreed with the behaviourist view that if new behaviour is to persist then some form of reinforcement is necessary.
- In another study, Bandura (1963) showed that seeing someone being punished for aggressive behaviour stopped children from imitating that behaviour. However, the children had in fact still learned the behaviour because when they were later asked to reproduce it and were rewarded for each aggressive act, they showed high levels of imitative aggression.
- The learning had remained latent. Reinforcement is a source of motivation and therefore may be needed for performance.

Examiner tip

It is good practice to reflect on the conclusion of studies. In an extended writing question, you need only present an overview of the study followed by 'this study shows that…' and the conclusion. Such information can be considered 'use of relevant information' — an AO2 skill.

Knowledge check 10

What term is given to the punishment that is received indirectly, when observing another person being punished for behaving in a certain way?

Examiner tip

Latent means 'hidden'. Latent learning means that you have learned something but you do not demonstrate (perform) the behaviour or show that you have learned it. The learning remains hidden.

Examiner tip

Because social learning theory is a bridge between the cognitive approach and the behaviourist approach, there is considerable overlap between SLT and these approaches. When discussing SLT, do not stray into other approaches (e.g. describing Skinner's studies with rats to illustrate reinforcement in learning). Any points in your discussion should clearly and unambiguously apply to SLT.

Strengths of social learning theory

- Social learning theory is better able to explain the learning of complex social behaviour such as gender role behaviour than models of learning based on simple reinforcement.
- Social learning theorists show that role models can make learning more efficient. The theory can explain quick learning and novel behaviour. For some learning, such as crossing a road, it is necessary to get the behaviour right the first time or at least very quickly.
- Observational learning has produced practical applications such as modelling (see below).
- By considering cognitive factors, social learning theory is less mechanistic than behaviourism, which focuses entirely on external events.

Limitations of social learning theory

- Research involving Bobo dolls in laboratory environments lacks ecological validity, making it difficult to generalise the findings to everyday situations.
- In emphasising external factors, biological factors are largely ignored.

Examiner tip

Use the key SLT terminology (e.g. model, imitation) in any answer to a question on SLT. This will help you keep within the approach and also conveys to the examiner that you are referring to SLT and not any other approach.

Application of social learning theory (examples)

Topic area	Application
Anxiety disorders	**Modelling** to treat disorders, e.g. showing a **model** interacting happily with a phobic object. A **vicarious** association is made between the positive feelings demonstrated and the object.
Gender development	Social learning theorists see gender-related behaviour as acquired by **reinforcement**, **modelling** and **imitation**.
Stress management	In stress inoculation training a **model** may be observed using behavioural and cognitive skills in stressful situations.

Summary

After studying this topic, you should be able to

- describe the assumptions (features) of social learning theory
- understand that SLT is concerned not only with observable behaviour but also with the cognitive processes involved in learning
- know and use key terminology of SLT
- describe the acquisition of behaviour through observation of others' behaviour
- explain how psychologists investigate observational learning
- evaluate SLT, providing supporting evidence for your argument
- discuss applications of SLT

Cognitive approach

Specification content

The focus in cognitive psychology on how thoughts influence behaviour. The information processing approach and how this applies to human behaviour and thought. The use of computer analogies in understanding behaviour.

The cognitive approach began to transform psychology during the 1950s and early 1960s. It was a reaction against the behaviourist stimulus–response approach and an attempt to look inside the 'black box'. For cognitive psychologists, it is the events within a person that must be studied if behaviour is to be fully understood. These internal events, which occur between stimulus and response, are known as mental processes.

Unlike behaviourists, cognitive psychologists believe that it is possible to study internal mental processes in an objective way and that insight into mental processes may be inferred from behaviour. In making these inferences, cognitive psychologists often rely on an analogy between the mind and a computer.

The basic assumptions or features of the cognitive approach are as follows:
- The study of internal mental processes or cognitive processes is important in understanding behaviour.
- Cognitive processes mediate between stimulus and response.
- Thoughts influence behaviour.
- Humans do not passively respond to their environment. The human mind actively processes the information received.
- Humans are **information processors** and this processing is similar to that of a computer, with the 'computer' here used as an **analogy** for the human mind.
- Internal mental processes can be investigated scientifically.

Cognitive psychology can be divided into three main areas:
(1) **Experimental cognitive psychology.** This uses the experimental method to investigate mental processes such as memory, attention and problem solving in normal healthy people. Responses are used to make inferences about mental processes, e.g. memory.
(2) **Cognitive neuropsychology.** This investigates mental processes in brain-damaged people, e.g. some people with brain injuries can understand language but cannot produce words, suggesting that different parts of the brain are involved.
(3) **Cognitive science.** This involves computer simulation of cognitive processes, e.g. 'general problem solver', a program that attempts to simulate the strategies active in human problem solving.

Using computer analogies to understand behaviour

The problem for cognitive psychologists is that the structure of the human brain does not reveal anything about psychological functioning, i.e. how we think, speak, remember etc. For this reason cognitive psychologists need an analogy to describe *how* the brain works — a comparison with the operation of something already understood. Computers provide a suitable analogy. Consequently:

- Computer terminology has been applied to human cognition, e.g. input, output, storage, information processing, bottom-up and top-down processing, serial and parallel processing.
- Similarities have been suggested in terms of coding (electrical impulses), use of a central processing unit for manipulating information and storage of information.

Limitations of the computer analogy

- It presents human cognition in a predictable and mechanical way.
- Information can be transferred from one computer to another — this does not happen with humans.
- The philosopher A. J. Ayer pointed out that it is difficult and perhaps naïve to 'allow machines an inner life, to credit them with feeling and emotion, to treat them as moral agents'.

Information processing and how this applies to human behaviour and thought

The information processing approach in psychology is based on the computer analogy. These models of thought and behaviour view cognitive operations as taking place in stages similar to computer processes, e.g. input, coding, storage, retrieval, decoding and output, e.g. Atkinson and Shiffrin's 'Multi-store Model of Memory'. The information processing approach to cognitive development investigates changes in cognitive processing that occur with age.

Strengths of the cognitive approach

- It is scientific and based on carefully controlled research. The use of computer models helps us to understand unobservable mental processes.
- It tackles areas previously neglected by the behaviourist approach (inside the 'black box').
- It bases its explanations firmly at a psychological level and avoids reductionist explanations of human behaviour.
- It has provided useful psychological applications (see table on p. 17).
- The approach has been integrated into other approaches, e.g. social learning theory and social cognition, in order to provide a more comprehensive understanding of some behaviours.

Limitations of the cognitive approach

- The information-processing metaphor of 'man as a machine' is seen as simplistic, ignoring emotional, motivational and social factors in human behaviour.

- The emphasis on laboratory experiments means that the findings may not reflect everyday behaviour.

- Much research and theory is highly specific, e.g. theories of attention, memory and perception. The approach lacks general theories that integrate the different parts of cognitive psychology into a coherent whole.

Application of the cognitive approach (examples)

Topic area	Application
Social cognition	Social **schemas** or **mental frameworks** represent information about oneself, other people and social situations. These help with **encoding** new information, focusing **attention**, influencing what is **remembered** and guiding behaviour.
Cognitive development	Piaget proposed stages of cognitive development which reflect the increasing sophistication of children's **thinking**. The **information-processing approach** sees children's minds as **computers** that gradually develop in **processing** ability.
Moral development	Piaget and Kohlberg proposed that moral development occurs in stages. The level of moral reasoning demonstrated by a child reflects its underlying stage of **cognitive** development.
Cognition and law	Theories of perceptual processing have been applied to explanations of face recognition: **top-down** and **bottom-up processing**. Knowledge of how **memory** works has been applied to interviewing witnesses, e.g. the cognitive interview.
Mood disorders	Beck's model of depression sees **faulty thinking** as the cause of depression. Ellis believes emotional and behavioural disorders develop because of **irrational beliefs** and **thoughts**.

Examiner tip
Students frequently state that the cognitive approach ignores emotion. This is not accurate and, while it certainly applies to the information processing approach, the cognitive approach does consider how cognitions and emotions interact in everyday life e.g. emotion and its effect on memory recall.

Summary

After studying this topic, you should be able to:
- describe the assumptions (features) of the cognitive approach
- understand that the cognitive approach focuses on the scientific study of internal mental processes
- know and use key terminology of the cognitive approach
- appreciate the breadth of cognitive psychology
- describe the related areas of cognitive psychology: experimental cognitive psychology; cognitive neuropsychology; cognitive science
- explain how cognitive psychologists investigate mental processes
- evaluate the cognitive approach, providing supporting evidence for your argument
- discuss applications of the cognitive approach

Psychodynamic approach

Specification content

Freud's approach to personality structure and dynamics. Unconscious mental processes. Psychosexual stages of development. Freud's use of case studies to highlight concepts. Erikson's theory and at least one other post-Freudian theory.

The term 'psychodynamic' means 'active mind' and implies active forces within the personality that motivate or 'drive' behaviour. Like the cognitive approach, it emphasises the inner causes of behaviour, though in the case of the psychodynamic approach, the focus is not on internal mental processes but on the unconscious conflict between the different structures that make up the whole personality. Freud's theory was the original psychodynamic theory and defines the approach. However, the approach also includes all those theories which are based on his ideas such as Erikson's, Jung's and Adler's.

Examiner tip

Because there are so many aspects to Freud's theory, think of three 'mini theories' that all interact: a theory of the structure of personality (id, ego, superego); a theory of personality dynamics (conscious and unconscious motivation and ego-defence mechanisms); and a theory of psychosexual development.

The basic assumptions or features of the psychodynamic approach are as follows:
- Much of our behaviour and feelings are **caused** by **unconscious** processes (**psychic determinism**).
- Behaviour is motivated by two basic **instincts.** These are the **life** and **death instincts** (**Eros** and **Thanatos**). These create **psychic** energy which causes tension and anxiety if it cannot be released.
- The different parts of the mind are in constant struggle (**psychodynamic conflict**).
- Behaviour and feelings as adults are rooted in childhood experiences.
- The sexual instinct or drive is active from birth and develops through a series of **psychosexual stages**. Personality is shaped as the child experiences conflicts at each stage.

Personality structure and dynamics

Personality is composed of three major systems:

Knowledge check 13

Explain why ego defence mechanisms are unconsciously motivated.

(1) **Id.** This consists of inherited instincts. It is entirely unconscious and operates according to the **pleasure principle**, selfishly seeking immediate gratification. It springs from two instinctive drives that all humans possess: **Eros**, which is fuelled by psychic energy called **libido**, and **Thanatos**.

(2) **Ego.** This is the rational and conscious part of the mind. The id's demands have to be satisfied but the ego takes into account the realities of life and tries to satisfy the instincts and reduce tension through rational activities. It operates according to the **reality principle.** If the id's demands cause anxiety, the ego may use **ego defence mechanisms** to relieve tension.

(3) **Superego.** This is the final part of personality to develop and represents the internalisation of the attitudes and values of the same-sex parent. It is mainly unconscious and operates according to the **morality principle**. It consists of two parts: the **ego-ideal**, which dictates what we should do and the **conscience**, which tells us what we should not do.

There is constant tension or 'dynamic' between the three aspects of personality. The ego acts as a mediator between the id and superego and seeks a compromise between id instincts and the moral demands of the superego. The unconscious conflicts between the three parts of personality motivate behaviour.

Unconscious mental processes

There are three layers of consciousness: the **conscious**, which contains present awareness; the **preconscious** which, although unconscious now, is capable of recall, and the **unconscious** part of the mind, which contains information that is almost impossible to bring into conscious awareness. It contains **repressed** thoughts, memories and wishes, id instincts, primitive desires and impulses. Defence mechanisms also operate at an unconscious level.

Freud saw the unconscious as a dynamic force which plays an important role in mental life. Its contents are kept out of awareness, not because they lack significance but because they are so significant that they threaten well-being.

Psychosexual stages of development

Personality develops through **psychosexual stages**, outlined in the table below. At each stage, libidinal energy is expressed in different ways and through varying parts of the body. If a child's needs at any of the stages are either unsatisfied or over-satisfied then **fixation** takes place. Behaviour patterns and problems from the fixated stage persist into adulthood. For example, a child fixated at the oral stage may show dependency as an adult and smoke or eat excessively.

Stage	Age	Outline
Oral	Birth–2 years	Child focuses on oral pleasures. Mouth is focal point of sensation.
Anal	2–3 years	Child focuses on pleasure associated with retaining and releasing faeces. Anus is focal point of sensation.
Phallic	3–6 years	Child focuses on genitals. Oedipus and Electra complexes resolved. Leads to gender identity.
Latent	6–12 years	Not really a psychosexual stage. Sexual desires are repressed; energies are channelled into social and intellectual development.
Genital	12+ years	Adult sexual interest.

Freud's use of case studies to highlight concepts

Freud's case studies can be used to illustrate his concepts. A well-known example is **Little Hans**. Hans was a 5-year-old boy who suffered from a phobia of horses, fearing that they would bite him. Freud's interpretation was that horses symbolised his father and the fear of biting represented **castration anxiety**. Hans had **unconscious** sexual desires for his mother, symptomatic of the **Oedipus complex.** Other case studies that can be used to highlight concepts include **Dora** and the **Rat Man**.

Examiner tip

Freud was very specific about the use of the term 'unconscious'. Make sure you use this term and not 'subconscious'. The 'unconscious' refers to material that contains repressed ideas, desires and impulses that have never been allowed to enter conscious awareness. The 'subconscious' is another word for the preconscious and consists of information that can be brought into consciousness.

Knowledge check 14

Explain what Freud meant by 'fixation'.

Examiner tip

Do not describe the psychosexual stages of development in detail in essay-type questions. Present descriptive content succinctly. The question usually requires you either to apply your knowledge of the approach or to evaluate it or compare it with another approach. In terms of descriptive content, only key points or an outline are needed.

Post-Freudian theories

Erikson placed less emphasis on innate sexual impulses and stressed the importance of the **ego** as well as **social** and **cultural** influences on psychological development. He proposed a series of **psychosocial stages** through which an individual passes during their lifetime. His **eight** stages each present a **crisis**, which needs to be sufficiently resolved in order to deal with the conflicts in subsequent stages. For example, in adolescence an individual must face the crisis of 'identity versus role-confusion'. Psychologically healthy individuals meet the challenges of each stage and grow in **ego strength**. Unlike Freud, Erikson believed that stages could be revisited and resolved at a later time.

Jung also attached less importance to sexuality and to childhood experiences. He emphasised the **collective unconscious**. This contains basic psychological truths which he called **universal archetypes**. These are shared by all human beings and come from our ancestral past. They predispose us in the same way as our ancestors, e.g. we do not learn to fear the dark or snakes — we are predisposed to such fears. Jung also proposed a different version of the libido — a force of greater and broader significance than merely sexual.

Adler agreed with Freud that personality is determined by unconscious wishes but did not agree with the idea of the pleasure principle. He believed that behaviour is driven by the desire to be **superior**. Conflict arises when the external environment is not compatible with the striving for perfection. Adler is responsible for the notion of the **inferiority** complex.

Strengths of the psychodynamic approach
- The psychodynamic approach has emphasised the importance of unconscious factors in determining behaviour.
- It draws attention to the importance of childhood experience on later behaviour.
- Freud's theory provided unique insight into human behaviour. The idea of unconscious motivation has gained widespread support among psychologists, as have defence mechanisms, internal conflicts and the irrational.
- The approach is still a major influence in psychology — especially in clinical areas of therapy. It has enormous explanatory power and has been applied to a wide variety of topics.

Limitations of the psychodynamic approach
- Freud's theory is largely derived from the study of adults with emotional disorders, an extremely unrepresentative sample.
- It is based on case studies and techniques that are subjective and open to bias.
- It is unscientific; it cannot be refuted. Psychologists who have tried to make predictions based on Freud's theory have generally not found support. Many concepts are vague and not operationally defined — another reason why the theory is difficult to verify.

- Freud's theory over-emphasises the role of instincts in human behaviour. It is unlikely that all of human behaviour is determined by sexual or aggressive drives that need to be released.
- Psychoanalytic therapy is difficult to evaluate. It is extremely long term and it is possible that someone might recover of their own accord during this period.
- Freud's theory, with its emphasis on instinctive, irrational human beings driven by the unconscious mind, is deterministic and pessimistic.

Application of the psychodynamic approach (examples)

Topic area	Application
Social cognition	The authoritarian personality is used to explain prejudice; **repressed** hostility towards parents is **displaced** onto another group.
Gender development	Successful identification with the same-sex parent at the end of the **Oedipus/Electra complexes** accounts for gender identity.
Remembering and forgetting	Traumatic memories are **repressed** in the **unconscious** mind.
Social development	Bowlby's theory of attachment sees the root of human personality in the **earliest relationships**. Erikson emphasised the importance of the **mother's** social responsiveness in the development of secure attachments and a sense of basic trust.
Anxiety disorders	Behaviour results from **unconscious repressed** traumatic memories and unresolved **childhood conflict**.

Examiner tip

When evaluating the psychodynamic approach, take care to distinguish between points that apply to the approach in general and points that are specific to Freud. For example, although Freud's theory is deterministic and pessimistic, the same cannot be said of Erikson, who presented a more positive and optimistic view of the human condition.

After studying this topic, you should be able to:

- describe the assumptions (features) of the psychodynamic approach
- understand that the psychodynamic approach focuses on unconscious mental processes
- know and use key terminology of the psychodynamic approach
- describe the related theories of Freud's psychodynamic approach
- describe Erikson's psychosocial theory and one other post-Freudian theory
- explain how Freud investigated mental processes
- evaluate the psychodynamic approach, providing supporting evidence for your argument
- discuss applications of the psychodynamic approach

Summary

Humanistic approach

Specification content

The person-centred approach of Rogers and Maslow. The importance within humanistic psychology of valuing individual experience, promoting personal growth, the concepts of free will and holism and the rejection of the traditional scientific approach.

Examiner tip
The humanistic approach stands in sharp contrast to many of the other approaches. These differences provide valuable discussion points for questions on both approaches and debates in psychology.

Humanistic psychologists reacted against the mechanical view of the person in behaviourism and the pessimistic and deterministic view presented by the psycho-dynamic approach. Instead, the stance they took was one of considering humans as free, essentially good and with the potential for growth and fulfilment.

The basic **assumptions/features** of the humanistic approach are as follows:

- Psychology should be concerned with the **subjective conscious** experience of the **individual** — the **person-centred** approach.
- Each individual is **unique**.
- The focus of understanding should be on the whole person — the **holistic** approach.
- Human beings have the freedom to choose their own destiny. They have **free will**.
- Human beings are seen as striving to achieve their potential or **self-actualisation** (to achieve maximum personal growth within individual limitations).
- **Scientific methods** are inappropriate for the study of human behaviour and experience.
- The aim of psychology should be to help people reach their full potential.

Person-centred approach of Rogers

- Rogers believed that people are born with a **self-actualising tendency**; an innate, ongoing drive towards achieving one's potential. Those able to self-actualise are **fully functioning persons**.
- People need **unconditional positive regard** (acceptance irrespective of behaviour), as opposed to conditional positive regard, which limits the development of the self.
- He emphasised the role of the **self-concept** which has three parts: the ideal self (what you want to be like); self-image (perceived self); self-esteem (self-worth). Good psychological health exists when there is a small gap between the ideal self and one's self-image. Low self-esteem also results from conditional positive regard of significant others.
- Rogers supported his theory with evidence from case studies of individuals he worked with during **person (client)-centred therapy.**
- Clients are encouraged to find their own solutions to their 'problems with living' and are responsible for their own destiny. The therapist is a facilitator (non-directive).
- The therapist provides warmth and unconditional positive regard. The aim is to improve the client's self-esteem and help him or her to become fully functioning.

Knowledge check 15
What term did Rogers use for the state of discomfort experienced when there is a significant gap between a person's self-image and ideal self?

Evaluation of Rogers' person-centred approach

- Rogers' person-centred therapy has had a major impact on psychotherapy and psychological thinking. His focus on the self-concept and the realisation of potential is of fundamental importance and perhaps more relevant than issues that have preoccupied more scientifically minded psychologists. However, from the standpoint of science, Rogers' ideas, like Freud's, are derived from therapy and are subjective.

Person-centred approach of Maslow

- People are essentially good with an inborn tendency towards growth and **self-actualisation** (achieving one's potential).
- Humans possess a range of motives for their behaviour. These can be divided into **deficiency motivation** (to maintain physical or psychological equilibrium) and **growth motivation** (refers to the tendency to self-actualise).
- The motives can be grouped together in a **hierarchy of needs.** Starting from the bottom, each need must be satisfied before the next can motivate us. At the top of the hierarchy is the need for self-actualisation. If people do not achieve this, they are likely to feel restless and dissatisfied with life.

Knowledge check 16

Identify two deficiency needs or motives.

Evaluation of Maslow's person-centred approach

- Maslow's theory provides an alternative to the deterministic psychodynamic and behaviourist approaches. It provides insight into what it means to be human and the hierarchy of needs is helpful in showing how human motives interact. It has been applied to education, therapy and management. However, like Rogers' theory, it is not based on scientific evidence and does not apply equally to all people (some people are unable to achieve self-actualisation).

Valuing individual experience

Humanistic psychologists emphasise the uniqueness of each individual and believe that:
- To really understand a person one needs to see things from that person's perspective. Rogers' therapy involved **empathetic** understanding.
- A person's subjective individual experience (phenomenology) is not to be questioned or challenged but should always be seen as valid.

Promoting personal growth

Humanistic psychologists regard personal growth as an essential part of what it means to be human. For Maslow, personal growth occurs when deficiency needs are satisfied, allowing for self-actualisation. Personal growth for Rogers occurs with the fully functioning person.

Free will and holism

Humanistic psychologists regarded individuals as active agents, able to influence their own development and possessing free will. Rogers' client-centred therapy places responsibility, free will and control in the hands of the client. Each person is seen as the best expert on himself or herself and best fitted to make decisions and solve his or her own problems.

Humanistic psychologists believe that the whole person should be studied and that it is essential to consider them and their behaviours in a holistic way. Maslow studied

Examiner tip
The specification identifies both Maslow and Rogers by name. Although they share the same fundamental humanistic assumptions, their theories differ. It is useful therefore to know the differences between their respective person-centred approaches, and be prepared to evaluate each theory.

Examiner tip
Even though Maslow and Rogers both believe that personal growth is a basic human motive essential to psychological health, they differ in their accounts of how personal growth occurs.

people from a holistic perspective, believing that a sense of fulfilment helps them feel more complete or 'whole'. Rogers used client-centred therapy to treat the entire individual.

Rejection of the scientific approach

There are several reasons why humanistic psychologists rejected the scientific approach:

- Belief in free will is incompatible with scientific (deterministic) approaches.
- A person's subjective conscious experience, not objective reality, is of primary concern.
- The scientific approach is unable to capture the richness of conscious experience. It is reductionist, not holistic.
- The scientific approach is dehumanising.

Examiner tip
Be prepared to explain each reason. For each, you need to demonstrate to the examiner that you understand why the features of science and the assumptions of the humanistic approach are at odds with one another.

Strengths of the humanistic approach

- It emphasises choice (free will) and responsibility — largely ignored by other approaches.
- It considers subjective conscious experience.
- It values personal ideals and self-fulfilment.
- It has enabled psychologists to explore human existence with more sensitivity than the more scientific methods.
- It has contributed to psychological theories and has been shown to be effective in the treatment of some disorders.

Limitations of the humanistic approach

- Partly because of its opposition to the scientific approach, the humanistic approach has had less impact on mainstream psychology than other approaches.
- The use of qualitative techniques has been questioned, particularly by psychologists who support a scientific approach.
- Because the subject matter is individual experience, it is not possible to formulate general laws of behaviour.
- Although the humanistic approach has provided valuable insight, terms such as 'self-actualisation' and the 'fully-functioning person' need precise definition. Because of the vagueness of such terms, little empirical research has been carried out.
- The humanistic approach puts too much emphasis on one drive: self-actualisation.
- The values championed by the humanistic approach have been criticised as being culture-bound. Not all cultures share the assumption that individual achievement brings fulfilment.

Examiner tip
Discussion of the humanistic approach can be quite difficult because the approach lacks supporting evidence. Additionally, the concepts are vague and abstract with fewer applications to topic areas. One strategy of developing the discussion or evaluation is to draw comparisons with other approaches.

Application of the humanistic approach (examples)

Topic area	Application
Mood disorders	Depression/**low self-esteem** result from lack of **unconditional positive regard** and an inability to accept one's self.
Schizophrenia	Humanistic therapies cannot directly tackle serious disorders but can be used as a supportive **therapy**, e.g. for relatives.

Topic area	Application
Schizophrenia	Milieu therapy (a half-way house for chronic institutionalised patients) involves the creation of an environment conducive to self-respect and **individual responsibility**.
Stress	Counselling for stressful life events such as divorce and bereavement allows clients insight and **control**.

After studying this topic, you should be able to:

- describe the assumptions (features) of the humanistic approach
- understand that the humanistic approach focuses on the subjective conscious experience of the individual
- know and use key terminology of the humanistic approach
- describe the person-centred approach of Maslow and Rogers

- understand why the humanistic approach conflicts with the scientific approach
- explain how humanistic psychologists investigated subjective conscious experience
- evaluate the humanistic approach, providing supporting evidence for your argument
- discuss applications of the humanistic approach

Summary

Comparison of approaches

Summary specification content

Comparison of biological, behaviourist, social learning theory, cognitive, psychodynamic and humanistic approaches. The extent to which the different approaches overlap and complement each other. The value of individual approaches and the merits of taking an eclectic approach to explaining human behaviour and in the application of psychology.

An eclectic approach involves adopting theories (and methods) from a range of approaches and putting these together in such a way as to produce a new hybrid theory. The new theory should eventually replace two or more approaches to provide a broader approach. Psychology has not yet reached such a stage, though this does not mean that psychologists cannot draw upon several approaches better to explain the subject matter at hand.

Strengths of adopting an eclectic approach

- Each person is unique and has different experiences. It is difficult to accommodate this fact with just one approach.
- A single approach results in an overly narrow view of human nature. An eclectic approach may provide a fuller, richer picture.
- Many topics in psychology can be better understood by integrating findings from several approaches, e.g. atypical disorders are often due to interacting biological, psychological and environmental factors.

Examiner tip

In questions on the eclectic approach, consider the approach with reference to methods, theory and practical applications.

Examiner tip

When evaluating an eclectic approach, consider the relevant strengths and weaknesses of the eclectic approach and use topics to illustrate the point.

- Theoretical unification would have implications for the status of psychology as a science.
- In the treatment of disorders, no one treatment is universally appropriate. A therapist may take a psychodynamic approach with one individual but a more direct cognitive approach with another.

Limitations of adopting an eclectic approach

- It is hard to combine information from different approaches into one theory.
- It is difficult to reconcile the individual contributions of each approach.

You are expected to make comparisons between the different approaches and to recognise that there is a degree of overlap between them. Some examples are given below. In considering the value of individual approaches, think of topic areas where the approaches offer different explanations for the same phenomenon, and whether or not these topics can be better understood by integrating findings from several approaches.

Examples of topic areas you may wish to consider are: gender, anxiety disorders, autism, schizophrenia, mood disorders, substance abuse and offending behaviour.

Comparisons, overlap and complementarities between the approaches

Approach	Nature of human beings	Overlap and complementarities
Biological	Behaviour determined by **genetic, physiological** and **neurobiological** factors. The influence of the **central nervous system** is crucial.	**Psychodynamic**: inheritance of instincts and evolution of human behaviour. **Cognitive**: cognitive neuropsychology.
Behaviourist	Behaviour controlled by the **environment**; it is learned, shaped and maintained by **reinforcement**.	**Psychodynamic**: role of early experience. **Social learning theory**: role of reinforcement.
Social learning theory	Behaviour learned through the **observation** of models.	**Behaviourist**: learning of behaviour and role of reinforcement. **Cognitive**: role of mental processes in learning.
Cognitive	People are **information processors**. Memory, perception and language are defining human characteristics.	**Biological**: cognitive neuropsychology. **Social learning theory:** cognitive factors.
Psychodynamic	Behaviour determined by **unconscious forces**. Conflicting demands made by the id, ego and superego.	**Behaviourist**: role and quality of experience. **Biological**: inheritance of instincts and evolution of behaviour.
Humanistic	Present **experience** is as important as past experience. People are **free** and rational.	**Biological**: innate tendency to realise one's potential. **Cognitive**: internal conscious experience.

Examiner tip

'Integrating' findings means 'joining together' or 'combining'. For a question on the value of individual approaches and the merits of integrating approaches, do not simply present a list of alternative explanations for a topic, but discuss how joining two or more approaches together might be a more effective explanation for a behaviour than relying on just one approach.

Examples of some key differences between the approaches

Approach	Issue	Comparison
Biological	**Atypical behaviour** is illness — due to genetic, physiological and neurobiological factors.	**Psychodynamic** approach: seen as determined by psychological factors, e.g. intrapsychic conflict. **Behaviourist** approach: seen as due to maladaptive learning.
Behaviourist	Role of **nurture**.	Behaviourists see nurture/ environment as the key to differences between people. The **psychodynamic** emphasises nature with a lesser role for nurture; for **cognitivists** nature and nurture interact.
Social learning theory	Research focus has been on **human behaviour**.	Other approaches use animals, e.g. the **biological approach** has investigated aggression and sex-related behaviour in animals while the **behaviourists** used rats and pigeons to study learning.
Cognitive	**Range** of study areas, e.g. cognitive processes and cognitive development.	**Behaviourism** has neglected many areas due to the limited focus on overt behaviour.
Psychodynamic	**Unconscious internal processes** are the key to understanding how we feel and behave.	The **humanistic approach** (focus on subjective experience) and the **cognitive approach** and **social learning theory** (focus on internal mediating processes) are also concerned with internal events. However, these focus on conscious processes.
Humanistic	People are basically **free** and responsible for their behaviour.	All other approaches take a determinist position, e.g. the **behaviourist approach** is entirely determinist while the **cognitive approach** adopts soft determinism.

Knowledge check 17

How did evolutionary theory influence Freud's psychodynamic theory?

Examiner tip

Make sure you can elaborate each comparative point in the tables. Explain each point with reference to the basic assumptions of the approaches and support with reference to topic areas and/or examples of behaviour.

After studying this topic, you should be able to:

- describe how some of the approaches in psychology overlap with each other
- describe how some of the approaches in psychology differ from each other
- discuss points of comparison with reference to topic areas and and/or examples of behaviour
- discuss the value of individual approaches vs. the merits of combining approaches to explaining human behaviour
- discuss the value of individual approaches vs. the merits of combining approaches in the application of psychology
- know what is meant by an 'eclectic approach'
- evaluate an eclectic approach, providing supporting evidence for your argument

Summary

Debates in psychology

Summary specification content

Free will and determinism. Nature–nurture. Holism and reductionism. Idiographic and nomothetic. Psychology and science.

Examiner tip
Notice that a definition of a debate includes both sides of the debate.

You are expected to be able to engage in the debates and to relate the different approaches in psychology to these issues. For psychology and science, you need to know the features and principles of the scientific approach and be able to relate the different approaches in psychology to the nature of scientific enquiry. Be prepared to draw on topic areas when discussing all the debates.

Free will and determinism

Specification content

Hard and soft determinism. Biological, environmental and psychic determinism. The scientific emphasis on causal explanations.

Examiner tip
Avoid defining 'determinism' in terms of 'behaviour is determined'. This produces a tautological answer for which you will not be credited. Use expressions such as 'behaviour is caused by...' or 'behaviour is a result of...' rather than 'determined'.

The **free will and determinism debate** is concerned with whether or not behaviour is freely produced by choice or whether it is caused by forces (internal or external) over which the individual has no control.

Types of determinism

Biological determinism

Biological determinism includes the controlling role of different parts of the brain, the hormonal system, evolutionary forces and genes on behaviour. Studies have indicated a genetic predisposition towards behaviours such as depression and schizophrenia.

Knowledge check 19
Name a brain structure that has been found to be linked to aggression.

Psychic determinism

Psychic determinism is represented by Freud's psychodynamic theory. Human behaviour, thoughts and feelings are determined (caused) by the life and death instincts and by repressed conflicts, wishes and memories in the unconscious mind. Because the causes of behaviour are unconscious, people believe that they are free.

Environmental determinism

Environmental determinism is the idea that behaviour is caused by factors within the external environment. Research into social influence (Asch 1955 and Milgram 1963) demonstrates the 'power of the situation' and how social factors can have a strong causal effect on behaviour. The behaviourist approach represents the extreme in environmental determinism. Behaviour is the product of prior reinforcements (positive and negative) and punishment. Skinner is well known for his assertion that free will is an illusion.

Issues raised by the debate

(1) Determinism accords with **the scientific emphasis on causal connections**. It assumes that all behaviour has a cause. If behaviour has a cause, it can also be predicted and controlled. Belief in determinism grants psychology the esteemed status of a science.

(2) If determinism implies that behaviour is caused, then the logical definition of free will might be that behaviour has no cause, is random and unpredictable. However, everyday experience does not support this view, yet, at the same time, people feel free to choose how they behave. William James used the term **soft determinism**, meaning that people have a choice (free will) yet at the same time, behaviour is to some extent predictable and does have a cause within the individual, e.g. their character or conscious goals. Soft determinism contrasts with **hard determinism**, the view that behaviour is caused by events entirely outside a person's control. According to this view, behaviour is both totally predictable and totally determined.

(3) If behaviour is externally caused, then an individual is not **responsible** for their behaviour. However, most people feel morally responsible for their actions and also hold others responsible for their actions. **Biological determinism** is sometimes put forward as an argument for the absence of moral responsibility.

Knowledge check 20

Which approach in psychology takes an extreme hard determinism position?

Different approaches and the free will and determinism debate

Approaches	Free will and determinism debate
Biological	**Determinism**: there are **biological** limitations on freedom of choice. There is also an element of **environmental determinism** because the environment is partly dictated by biological factors.
Behaviourist	**Environmental determinism**: there are no choices. Behaviour is totally determined by reinforcement and punishment.
Social learning theory	Environment determines behaviour and behaviour determines the environment (different individuals seek out different experiences). Because a person reasons when deciding how to act and exercises **choice**, there is an element of **soft determinism**. Bandura calls mutual interaction between person, behaviour and environment **'reciprocal determinism'**.
Cognitive	**Soft determinism**: people select what to attend to etc. so choose their thoughts and behaviour, but these choices are determined by innate capabilities and past experience.
Psychodynamic	**Unconscious** or **psychic determinism**: behaviour is determined by unconscious forces, although the reasons for behaviour are explained by the conscious mind.
Humanistic	**Free will**: people direct their lives towards self-chosen goals, as seen in humanistic-based therapies.

Examiner tip

When planning a discussion on the debate, think whether the behaviours covered under the topic areas are a result of free will or determinism. Back up your points with reference to studies, theories and approaches in psychology. Do not think of the debate in terms of strengths and limitations of the two sides.

Possible topic areas to include in a discussion

Topic area	Application
Obedience to authority	Milgram's participants claimed that they had **no choice** but to obey, they were in an 'agentic state'. However they were seen as **responsible** for their behaviour and had the option to disobey.
Offending behaviour	Most theories of offending include some elements of **determinism**. How is such a view reconciled with the punishment of offenders?
Therapies for psychological disorders	In humanistic client-centred therapy, the client consciously and rationally decides what to do about his/her condition, in stark contrast with all other 'directive' therapies, which take a **deterministic** view.

> **Examiner tip**
> Notice that, in the table, for every topic applied to the debate, the two positions are presented. This is the approach you should take if asked to discuss the debate.

> **Summary**
> After studying this topic, you should be able to:
> - outline and explain what is meant by biological, environmental and psychic determinism
> - distinguish between hard and soft determinism
> - explain why the ideas of determinism are compatible with the scientific method
> - understand some of the problems with belief in free will for psychology
> - apply the free will and determinism debate to the approaches in psychology
> - apply the free will and determinism debate to topics in psychology

> **Examiner tip**
> Take an analytical look at this definition. 'Relative contribution' means that both nature and nurture are essential to understand and explain any behaviour. Avoid any suggestion that you think the debate is about explanations of behaviour as being 'either' heredity 'or' environment.

> **Examiner tip**
> Students sometimes state that 'nature is determinism and nurture is free will'. This possibly stems from the association between determinism and the biological approach and is an oversimplification. The behaviourist approach rejects the role of free will in behaviour. Similarly, genetic evidence is not automatically accepted in mitigation for a crime.

Nature–nurture debate

Specification content

The relative importance of heredity and environment in determining behaviour. An interactionist approach.

The **nature–nurture** debate is concerned with the relative contributions of nature (**heredity**) and nurture (**environment**, experience and learning) to behaviour. The roots of the debate lie in **philosophy**. The nature side of the debate is associated with **nativist** theory; the nurture side with **empiricist** theory. Nativists stressed inherited influences on behaviour whereas empiricists believed that knowledge results mainly from learning and experience. The British philosopher, John Locke, believed that at birth, the human mind is simply a blank slate or *tabula rasa* which is gradually filled in by experience and learning from the environment. Nowadays the thrust of the debate is on an **interactionist approach** — the belief that *both* nature *and* nurture are essential to any behaviour and interact in a complex manner.

The classic example of the interaction between heredity and environment is that of **phenylketonuria (PKU).** This condition is due to a pair of defective genes and can result in brain damage. However, if it is detected soon after birth and the child is raised on special diet, development is normal. So although PKU is hereditary, it is not possible to separate nature and nurture. One cannot say that **genetic** factors caused brain damage and low intelligence; neither can it be claimed that the **environment** caused brain damage and low intelligence.

Investigating the genetic basis of behaviour

(1) The **heritability estimate** represents the extent to which a characteristic is genetic in origin. It provides a numerical value from 0 to 1.0; the greater the value, the greater the role of genes. The heritability estimate only refers to genetic factors in **variability** among individuals.

(2) One way of establishing the genetic basis of behaviour is to use **twin studies.** The purpose of twin studies is to 'separate out' the relative contributions of heredity and environment. Monozygotic (MZ) twins share the same genes; dizygotic (DZ) twins have 50% of their genes in common. If MZ twins reared together are more alike than DZ twins reared together (for the behaviour under investigation), then any increased similarity must be genetic. The degree of agreement is expressed as a **concordance rate**. Twin studies of intelligence and schizophrenia typically show higher concordance rates for MZ twins, suggesting genetic influence.

(3) **Adoption studies** are also used to investigate the genetic basis of behaviour. If adopted individuals are found to be more similar to their biological parents on some measure than to their adoptive parents, this suggests that genes are more influential than environment. Adoption studies have investigated the role of genes in disorders including depression, alcoholism and schizophrenia.

> **Knowledge check 21**
>
> Explain what is meant by concordance.

Evaluation

- Even MZ twins reared together do not show perfect concordance rates, leading some psychologists to focus on the unshared environments of siblings.
- MZ twins often share a more similar environment than DZ twins. To counter this, psychologists have studied MZ twins separated early in life.
- MZ twins separated early in life are quite rare and any 'different environments' are in fact often quite similar.

> **Knowledge check 22**
>
> Why is it not possible to establish cause and effect in twin studies and adoption studies?

Different approaches and the nature–nurture debate

Approaches	Nature–nurture debate
Biological	The focus is on **heredity**, though the interaction with environment is acknowledged. Nature interacts with nurture.
Behaviourist	Behaviourists emphasise **nurture**; behaviour is directly shaped and controlled by the **environment**.
Social learning theory	Social learning theorists stress the role of the **environment** but also consider interaction between the individual and their environment.
Cognitive	Cognitive psychologists are **interactionist**, e.g. Piaget proposed that **innate** schemas develop through continuous **interaction** with the world.
Psychodynamic	The focus is on the **inherited** instinctual drives of sex and aggression. Freud also acknowledged the influence of different experiences during the psychosexual stages of development. **Nurture**, though, is always secondary.
Humanistic	Life's main motive, the need to self-actualise, is **innate**. However, humans are influenced by **environmental** variables, e.g. unconditional positive regard and favourable growth conditions.

> **Examiner tip**
>
> Make sure that you can discuss each approach. You could refer to research, theories, topics etc. For example, for the humanistic approach you could refer to the fact that few people achieve self-actualisation at the top of the hierarchy of needs, illustrating the role of nurture interacting with the innate need to self-actualise.

Possible topic areas to include in a discussion

Topic area	Discussion
Perceptual processes	The Gestalt psychologists believed that the basic principles of perceptual organisation were **innate**. Perceptual set and the effects of culture and expectation involved **experience**.
Schizophrenia	The diathesis-stress model suggests an **innate** susceptibility to the disorder which can be triggered by **environmental** stress — a good example of **interaction** between heredity and environment.
Gender	Case studies and cross-cultural studies contribute to discussion about the roles of **nature** and **nurture** in gender development.

Summary

After studying this topic, you should be able to:

- understand what psychologists mean by the nature–nurture debate
- explain what is meant by an 'interactionist' approach in the context of the nature–nurture debate
- explain how psychologists investigate the genetic basis of behaviour
- discuss some of the methodological problems in investigating the genetic basis of behaviour
- apply the nurture–nature debate to the approaches in psychology
- apply the nurture–nature debate to topics in psychology

Reductionism and holism

Specification content

The strengths and limitations of reductionist and holistic explanations. An interactionist approach.

Reductionism in psychology has two related meanings:

- Breaking down complex phenomena into separate components in order to explain and understand behaviour, e.g. explaining face recognition as the result of processing the sum of facial features.
- Reducing explanations of behaviour to simpler levels, e.g. attempting to explain behaviour in terms of neurophysiology, biochemistry or genetics.

Holistic explanations emphasise the whole of behaviour or experience rather than the individual components, e.g. explaining face recognition in terms of facial features, the context in which the face is seen, the feelings the face evokes, its expressions etc.

Example of a reductionist explanation of behaviour

Some psychologists have attempted to explain **schizophrenia** in terms of the activity of the **neurotransmitter** dopamine or the influence of **genes.** This is simpler than considering social and environmental factors. Such higher level explanations and the interactions between them are not readily observable nor easily defined or measured.

Strengths of reductionist explanations

- Reductionism works on the scientific principle of parsimony (economical explanation) and is consistent with a scientific approach to psychology.
- Breaking phenomena down into smaller, simpler components means that these can be more easily tested and theories falsified or verified.
- Reductionism links psychology to respected scientific disciplines such as biology and neuroscience.
- By simplifying behaviour, reductionism makes it easier for behaviour to be explained in concrete and concise terms.

Limitations of reductionist explanations

- The complexity of behaviour is missed. Reductionist explanations often ignore many important interactions.
- Behaviour often derives its meaning from the context in which it occurs, e.g. depression is perhaps better understood in the context in which it occurs rather than when explained in terms of neurotransmitters.
- Reductionist explanations may distract attention from other types of explanation, e.g. explaining intelligence at the level of genes means that opportunities to stimulate and enrich may be missed.

Example of holistic explanations of behaviour

A Gestalt view of learning, which is opposed to the reductionist S–R approach, is 'insight learning' as demonstrated by Kohler (1925). A banana and a stick were placed outside the cage of a hungry chimpanzee. The stick was positioned within reach but the banana was out of reach. After unsuccessfully trying to grasp the banana there was a pause in activity, then suddenly the chimpanzee reached for the stick and used it to rake in the banana. Insight learning happens when all elements (in this study — stick, arm and distances) are seen in **relationship to each other** and thus form a **meaningful whole**. Insight learning could not be explained simply by behaviourist S–R connections and reinforcement.

An interactionist approach

This approach integrates **several** levels of explanation to provide a more complete understanding of behaviour. In explaining schizophrenia, for example, **biological**, **psychological** and **social** factors are considered. Social factors can extend to society as a whole and not just a person's immediate social group. Only by taking account of **all** these factors can psychologists get a better understanding of the problem.

> **Examiner tip**
> In preparing for the exam, consider reductionist attempts to explain and understand behaviour in the topics you have studied. Is greater insight into behaviour achieved by considering the sum of the components of behaviour/reducing explanations of behaviour to simpler and lower levels? Or is such reductionism an oversimplification of behaviour?

> **Knowledge check 24**
> In the context of the holism–reductionism debate in psychology, what is meant by 'higher-level explanations'?

> **Examiner tip**
> Be absolutely clear about what the issue is in this debate. The argument is not about whether reductionist explanations such as biological processes play a role in behaviour but whether such explanations alone can provide insight into complex behaviour.

> **Examiner tip**
> Notice that an interactionist approach is by definition holistic.

Strengths of holistic and interactionist explanations

- Compared with reductionist explanations, holistic and interactionist explanations may provide a more complete picture.
- Holistic and interactionist explanations do not ignore the complexity of behaviour and thus can be more meaningful.
- Behaviour is variable and determined by many factors, so interactionist explanations may be more helpful than reductionist ones.

Limitations of holistic and interactionist explanations

- It is difficult to investigate how different types and levels of explanation are integrated.
- Holistic explanations are more hypothetical than lower-level reductionist explanations and theories lack the predictive power of a scientific explanation.

Different approaches and the holism and reductionism debate

Approaches	Holism and reductionism debate
Biological	Explanations at the level of **genes**, **hormones**, **neurochemistry** and **brain activity** are **reductionist** and often regarded as incomplete accounts of behaviour.
Behaviourist	Behaviourists argue that simple stimulus and response links (S–R links) are the appropriate unit of analysis. Complex behaviour can be **reduced** to a series of behavioural S–R links.
Humanistic	Humanistic psychologists believe that a person can only be understood as a **whole**. Thoughts, behaviour and experience should not be reduced to smaller component elements.

Possible topic areas to include in a discussion

Topic area	Discussion
Face recognition	According to **holistic** theory, a face is recognised as a **whole** and not by simple analysis of its component features. In contrast, feature analysis theory is **reductionist**.
Schizophrenia	Socio-cultural explanations (labelling and family dysfunction) are **higher level** and more **holistic** than the biological explanations which are **reductionist**.
Perceptual processes	Visual illusions, e.g. the Müller-Lyer, demonstrate that people perceive more than the **sum** of sensations on the retina.

Summary

After studying this topic, you should be able to:

- understand what psychologists mean by reductionist and holistic explanations of behaviour
- explain what is meant by an interactionist approach in the context of the holism–reductionism debate
- evaluate reductionist and holistic explanations of behaviour
- apply the reductionism–holism debate to the approaches in psychology
- apply the reductionism–holism debate to topics in psychology

Idiographic and nomothetic approaches

Specification content

The strengths and limitations of idiographic versus nomothetic research.

An **idiographic** view takes the position that everyone is **unique**. This approach involves psychological analysis of **individual** cases as a means of understanding behaviour.

Features and methods of research

Idiographic

- The focus is on the **individual** and the recognition of their **uniqueness**.
- It is concerned with private, **subjective** and conscious experiences of the individual.
- Methods of research tend to involve **qualitative data**, investigating individuals in a personal and detailed way. Numerical measurement is not excluded but the main emphasis is on description.
- Methods of research include: the case study, which can provide a global understanding of the individual; unstructured interviews; self-reports; autobiographies and also personal documents such as diaries and letters.

Strengths of idiographic research

- The idiographic approach provides a more complete or global understanding of the individual than the nomothetic approach.
- It satisfies a key aim of science — the description and understanding of behaviour. In so doing, it complements the nomothetic approach.
- Its findings can serve as a source of ideas or hypotheses for later study.

Limitations of idiographic research

- Generalisations cannot be made to a wider population.
- Methods of research tend to be subjective and unstructured, causing problems for analysis, replication, prediction and control of behaviour.
- It is not possible to use statistical analysis in small-scale research, which mainly collects qualitative data.
- The idiographic approach is regarded as unscientific.

A **nomothetic** view involves studying large numbers of people, trying to understand why they behave in similar ways in certain situations. It is concerned with developing **general laws** of behaviour.

> **Examiner tip**
> Do not get sidetracked into details of the humanistic approach and client-centred therapy when answering a question on the idiographic approach. Although the idiographic approach is exemplified by aspects of the humanistic approach, its scope extends beyond the confines of one particular approach.

> **Examiner tip**
> It is important to be able to 'discuss' or elaborate any of the points you raise. You may notice that the reference to the scientific approach appears as both a strength and a limitation. You could exploit this tension to promote an interesting discussion.

Knowledge check 25

What is meant by 'objective knowledge'?

Examiner tip

If asked for a strength of an approach, do not simply give a feature of the approach. State 'the strength is…' and give a reason. This will ensure focus on the question. Alternatively you could compare the approaches in order to bring out a strength.

Features and methods of research

Nomothetic

The focus is on **similarities** between people and general **laws** of behaviour that can be applied to **large populations**.

- It is concerned with **objective** knowledge.
- General laws can be of three kinds (Radford and Kirby 1975):
  - **Classifying** people into groups, e.g. Diagnostic and Statistical Manual of Mental Disorders (DSM-IV) classifies people suffering from psychological disorders.
  - **Establishing principles** of behaviour that can be applied to people in general, e.g. behaviourist laws of learning.
  - **Establishing dimensions** on which people can be placed, e.g. Eysenck's personality inventory (EPI) gives personality scores that allow for comparisons between people.

Nomothetic research uses **scientific** and **quantitative data**, usually **experiments** and **observations**. Group averages can be statistically analysed and predictions made about people in general.

Strengths of nomothetic research

- The nomothetic approach is regarded as scientific.
- Scientific principles which feature in the nomothetic approach are: precise measurement; prediction and control of behaviour; investigations involving large groups; objective and controlled methods which allow for replication and generalisation.

Limitations of nomothetic research

- Predictions can be made from group results but these may not apply to every person; the approach has been accused of losing sight of the 'whole person'.
- The nomothetic approach gives a superficial understanding. Two people may have achieved the same score on a test of intelligence but they may have arrived at that score in quite different ways.

Idiographic and nomothetic approaches working together

Both approaches have a role in psychology, but the relative value of each depends on the **purpose of the research**. It makes sense to use the nomothetic approach when studying behaviour in general and the idiographic approach to understand and predict a particular person's behaviour.

The two approaches can be **complementary**. The idiographic approach can shed further light on a general law of behaviour established through a nomothetic approach. The idiographic approach can also unearth issues which can then be explored, through a nomothetic approach, for their potential for a wider application.

Both approaches can contribute to the **scientific approach**; the idiographic being more suited to description and understanding of behaviour, the nomothetic to prediction and control of behaviour.

Different approaches and their relation to nomothetic and idiographic approaches

Approaches	Nomothetic and idiographic approaches
Biological	Mainly **nomothetic** — biological influences apply generally to all. However, the **idiographic** approach can complement the nomothetic approach — single cases can be informative.
Behaviourist	**Nomothetic** — general principles, identified using rigorous laboratory experimentation, applied to all organisms.
Social learning theory	**Nomothetic** — the establishment of general laws or principles of behaviour.
Cognitive	Mostly **nomothetic** — seeking to discover general principles/theories of cognitive processing but has also used **idiographic** techniques.
Psychodynamic	The case study method is clearly **idiographic**, yet Freud's theory of personality was applied to all — and is thus **nomothetic**.
Humanistic	**Idiographic** — emphasises the uniqueness of the individual.

Possible topic areas to include in a discussion

Topic area	Application
Cognitive development	Piaget used the **idiographic** approach, gaining rich and detailed information about the development of his children's thinking. These findings inspired further **nomothetic** research.
Social development	Bowlby's theory/research into maternal deprivation using the **nomothetic** approach has been challenged by case studies.
Remembering and forgetting	**Case studies** show how memory function is affected by brain damage. They have **complemented** the **nomothetic** approach, shedding light on general laws of behaviour and posing challenges.

Examiner tip

Case studies might generate hypotheses but in themselves are not tests of hypotheses. You must be cautious how you deploy evidence based on a case study alone.

Knowledge check 26

Evaluate Freud's use of the case study method (idiographic) to develop general laws of behaviour (nomothetic).

Summary

After studying this topic, you should be able to:

- explain what psychologists mean by idiographic and nomothetic approaches
- understand what is meant by idiographic and nomothetic approaches being 'complementary'
- evaluate idiographic and nomothetic approaches in psychology
- apply idiographic and nomothetic approaches to the approaches in psychology
- apply idiographic and nomothetic approaches to topics in psychology

Psychology and science

Specification content

The features and principles of the scientific approach: paradigm, the role of theory, hypothesis testing, empirical methods, replication and generalisation. Overt behaviour versus subjective, private experience. The role of peer review in validating research. Strengths and limitations of the scientific approach in psychology.

The features and principles of the scientific approach are as follows:
- There must be a **definable subject matter** or **paradigm**.
- There must be **theory** construction, from which **hypotheses** are derived and tested.
- Science should attempt to discover **general laws** or principles.
- **Empirical** methods of investigation are used to gather information.

Paradigm

Knowledge check 27

Identify a key theoretical difference between the humanistic approach and behaviourist approach.

Kuhn (1970) argues that a subject can only be called a science if there is an agreed common 'global' theory or paradigm. He believes that at present psychology is not characterised by a paradigm — that it is still a **pre-science**, because there are too many conflicting theoretical approaches and methods of enquiry and no one unifying theory.

Evaluation

Most psychologists agree about the overall subject matter of psychology: the study of mind and behaviour. Some, e.g. Palermo (1971), argue that psychology has progressed beyond the stage of 'science' and gone through several paradigm shifts (changes), e.g. behaviourism has recently been replaced by cognitive psychology, probably the dominant area of research today.

Role of theory and hypothesis testing

A theory is an explanation of facts and observations using a set of general principles. Theories are a necessary part of science for several reasons:
- Theories provide **understanding** and **explanation** by **organising** facts, finding **regularities** and reducing these to a short list of general principles.
- Theories provide the basis for research, generating **predictions** or **testable hypotheses**.
- The process of deriving new testable hypotheses from the theory is known as the **hypothetico-deductive method**. If the predictions are not confirmed when tested, then the theory is not supported. If the predictions are confirmed, then the theory is supported.

Examiner tip

Take care over use of terminology. Theories are 'supported' or 'not supported'. Do not write 'proved'/'proven'. Similarly, hypotheses are 'accepted' or 'rejected'.

A good scientific theory should be: a source of new hypotheses; testable; falsifiable; subject to attempts at refutation (capable of being 'shown to be wrong') and parsimonious (accounting for all the known facts in an economical way).

AQA(B) A2 Psychology

Empirical methods and replication

A theory that has not been subjected to **empirical** investigation cannot claim to be scientific. **Empirical methods** refer to methods of conducting research through **direct experience**, preferably (but not only) concerning the experiment itself. Information gathered should be **factual**, **verifiable** and **objective**. 'Empirical evidence' covers any evidence that is open to public scrutiny.

Empirical studies should be reported in detail because the scientific approach involves **replication**. This means that, when following the same procedure on different occasions, the findings of a study should be repeated (the results will be the same or similar). Replication may be harder to achieve in psychology than in other sciences because the subject matter involves human behaviour.

Replicability is an important feature of science because it enables theories to be strengthened, the **validity** of the findings to be supported, **generalisability** of the findings to be increased and the **practical value** (application) of theories to be improved.

Generalisation

Generalisation refers to the ability of the researcher to apply the findings from the sample in a particular study to other members of the target population and other situations. In order to generalise, the sample must be **representative** of the target population and the results of the investigation should apply beyond the immediate setting to other settings. This is known as **ecological validity**.

Overt behaviour and subjective private experience

Overt behaviour is behaviour that is **open** and **detectable**, and so amenable to scientific enquiry. It can include internal processes that cannot be directly observed but can be inferred from observable responses. More scientifically oriented approaches, e.g. behaviourist, biological and cognitive approaches, rely on overt behaviour in their investigations.

Subjective private experience is **internal** and **unique** to the individual. It is not easily investigated using scientific techniques and cannot be fully accessed nor replicated. Humanistic psychologists investigate unique, subjective, private experience believing this to be important in understanding the essential nature of human beings.

Role of peer review in validating research

In any science, theories and research findings have to be communicated through journals and conferences to other scientists in the field. Peer review plays a crucial role in:

(1) Validating the quality of research. Impartial specialists assess the quality of research, ensuring that hypotheses, methods and analysis of data were appropriate and that the conclusions were correct. Reviewers may suggest minor revisions or may reject the work as inappropriate for publication.

Examiner tip

'Lack of ecological validity' is perhaps the most overused evaluative point offered by students. Unless you can state why research lacks ecological validity, do not refer to it.

Knowledge check 28

Give some examples of how biological and cognitive psychologists study 'overt behaviour'.

(2) **Evaluating** research proposals. The peer review process helps to identify projects that are worthy of financial support from funding bodies. Projects should be well-designed, of technical merit, viable and relevant.

Strengths of the scientific approach in psychology

- It has respectability due to its scientific status.
- The scientific approach is objective and provides findings that are reliable and can be generalised.
- Because theories are an essential feature of the scientific approach, they provide general laws of behaviour and allow psychology to progress as a science.
- The scientific approach has resulted in applications which can improve people's lives and help solve problems.

Limitations of the scientific approach in psychology

- Because the subject matter in psychology is the behaviour of human beings, participants' expectations may influence the results (demand characteristics).
- Ethical restrictions may constrain psychological research. Some studies have to be adapted or abandoned despite their scientific value.
- Scientific methods strive for objectivity and control but this can result in an artificial environment which has implications for generalisability.
- It is difficult to control all variables that underlie human behaviour so totally accurate prediction is not possible.
- The scientific approach is deterministic and reductionist, ignoring the role of free will and destroying the 'totality' of human experience.
- Much of the subject matter of psychology is unobservable and cannot be accurately measured, only inferred.

Summary

After studying this topic, you should be able to:
- describe the features of the scientific approach
- understand the role of theory and hypothesis testing
- know the difference between overt behaviour and private subjective experience
- discuss whether or not psychology is a science
- understand the role of peer review in validating research
- apply the scientific approach to approaches and topic areas in psychology
- evaluate the use of the scientific approach in psychology

Methods in psychology

Inferential statistics

Summary specification content

The concepts of probability and levels of significance. Use of critical values in testing for significance. Hypothesis testing: One- and two-tailed tests. Type I and Type II errors. Positive, negative and zero correlation. Limitations of sampling techniques and generalisation of results.

At AS, the statistical procedures you were introduced to were concerned with summarising or describing information.

At A2 you need to move on to statistics, which enable prediction on the basis of limited information. Statistical procedures or statistical tests are applicable to all kinds of scientific work and you will be tested on your knowledge and understanding of these in the exam. You should keep a detailed record of any statistical analysis you have carried out in your lessons to help you prepare for the exam.

Inferential statistics allow the researcher to estimate the extent to which the results of an experiment or study could have occurred by chance. Inferences or conclusions about the target population can be drawn from the sample data.

Probability and levels of significance

We can never be 100% sure that the results of a study are not due to chance. We can only establish the **probability** or likelihood of this being the case.

The **level of significance** indicates the extent to which a set of results is due to chance. The level of significance is determined by carrying out an appropriate inferential (statistical) test and calculating an **observed** value for the data. This is then compared with the appropriate **critical** value found in a statistical table for the test.

Examiner tip
This unit builds on knowledge of 'Research Methods' acquired in Unit 1. Make sure you revisit this section. It is legitimate to be asked questions from this part of the specification at A2.

Knowledge check 29
Give two examples of descriptive statistics.

Examiner tip
Practice at reading tables of critical values (statistical tables) is recommended.

Common levels of significance

0.1% (Low or 'stringent' level of significance)	$p = 0.001$	Highly significant	Used in important research where chance must be minimised.
1%	$p = 0.01$	Very significant	May be used when challenging previous research findings.
5%	$p = 0.05$	Significant	**Conventional** and accepted **minimal level** of significance.
10% (High or 'lenient' level of significance)	$p = 0.1$	Not significant	May be worth doing follow-up studies.

The minimum level of significance is the 5% level — if the results are significant at the 5% level it means that they would have occurred by chance less than five times

out of a hundred. This is usually written as **$p < 0.05$**. At this level, the results are very unlikely to have occurred by chance alone (i.e. the probability of chance is low). Such results are often referred to as **significant**.

The level of significance should be specified before testing begins.

Hypothesis testing

Statistical tests test hypotheses. Before a study is conducted, the researcher formulates a null hypothesis and an alternative hypothesis. The alternative hypothesis predicts that an effect will occur and that the results will be significant. The alternative hypothesis is also referred to as the research hypothesis (or experimental hypothesis if the method used is an experiment).

Statistical tests give the probability of any effect being due to chance.

If this is less than the specified significance level (usually 5%), then the alternative hypothesis can be accepted and the null rejected.

If the alternative hypothesis predicts an effect in a specified direction (directional or **one-tailed hypothesis**), then the test of this hypothesis is known as a **one-tailed test**.

An example of a one-tailed hypothesis is, 'children will take *less* time to complete a numeracy task if they eat breakfast than if they go without breakfast'.

If the alternative hypothesis predicts an effect but does not specify the direction (non-directional hypothesis or **two-tailed hypothesis**), then the test of this hypothesis is a **two-tailed test**.

An example of a two-tailed hypothesis is, 'children will *differ* in the time taken to complete a numeracy task depending on whether or not they have eaten breakfast'.

It is important to know whether or not the hypothesis is one-tailed or two-tailed because this has implications for the outcome of the findings.
- It is twice as difficult to achieve a significant result with a two-tailed test as with a one-tailed test.
- If a one-tailed test is used and an effect is found in the opposite direction to that predicted, then the results are not significant.

How to decide on the type of hypothesis

Use a one-tailed hypothesis if there is evidence from previous research to predict the direction of results. This will be evident in the description of a study if you see phrases such as 'previous research has shown', 'the researcher expected' or 'on the basis of previous evidence it was predicted that'.

Use a two-tailed hypothesis if the evidence from previous research is conflicting. This will be evident in the description of a study if there is no reference to past research or predicted direction, or if the evidence is described as conflicting.

Type I and Type II errors

By stating that the level of significance is 5%, we are accepting that there is a 5% likelihood of chance.

A **Type I error** occurs if the null hypothesis is rejected but the results are due to chance. The effect was in fact caused by some random or uncontrolled variable. The researcher has made an optimistic error believing that there was a real (significant) effect rather than a chance occurrence.

It may help you to remember this as 'optimistic = one' (Type I/one).

A **Type II error** occurs if the null hypothesis is retained but the results are not due to chance. This can be the result of a poor research design, faulty sampling or a random error.

The more stringent (low) the level of significance, the more likely a Type II error. The more lenient (high) the level of significance, the less likely a Type II error and the greater the risk of a Type I error. The 0.05 level offers a sensible balance between the risks of a Type I and a Type II error.

Positive, negative and zero correlation

Correlation statistics express the strength of a **relationship** between two variables as a number between –1 and +1. This number is known as a **correlation coefficient**. **Scattergrams** are a way of illustrating correlational data.

There are three types of correlation:

(1) A **positive correlation** — as scores on one variable increase, so do scores on the other variable, e.g. the more time spent on psychology homework, the higher the final grade. A perfect correspondence gives a correlation coefficient of +1. Perfect correlations are rare in psychology but the closer the correlation coefficient is to 1 (e.g. +0.8 or +0.9), the stronger the relationship. A positive correlation is illustrated in Figure 1 below.

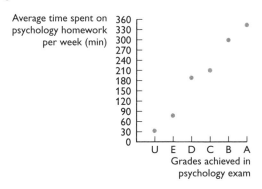

Figure 1 Scattergram showing a positive relationship

(2) A **negative correlation** — as scores on one variable increase, scores on the other variable decrease, e.g. the more time spent on psychology homework, the fewer parties attended. A perfect correspondence gives a correlation coefficient of –1. The closer the correlation coefficient is to –1 (e.g. –0.8 or –0.9), the stronger the relationship. A negative correlation is illustrated in Figure 2.

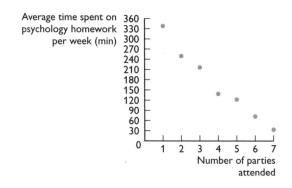

Figure 2 Scattergram showing a negative relationship

(3) A **zero correlation** — there is no relationship. No relationship at all is expressed by a correlation coefficient of 0. An example might be the time spent on psychology homework and shoe size. This is illustrated in Figure 3 below.

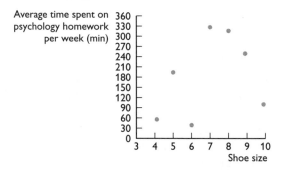

Figure 3 Scattergram showing a zero relationship — points are all over the place

Limitations of sampling techniques and generalisation of results

Generalisability of results refers to whether the results from a **sample** can be applied to the **target population** from which the sample is taken. The researcher must try to reduce **bias** in **samples**. This can be done by avoiding small samples and selecting **sampling techniques** which best represent the target population. This is not always easy. Even if a representative sample is selected, people can refuse to take part. Also, it is not always possible or appropriate to select a representative sample, e.g. when researching abortion or substance abuse.

Sampling techniques

Opportunity sample: people selected are those who are easily available and appear suitable for the investigation. This method is quick and convenient.

AQA(B) A2 Psychology

Limitations

- The participants may be a narrow group of very similar people. The sample is therefore unlikely to be representative, making it difficult to generalise.
- Selector bias may occur, where the researcher chooses whoever he or she wants to take part, such as friends or colleagues.

Random sample: every member of the target population has an equal chance of being selected. This can be done by drawing names from a hat or by giving everyone a number and using a computer or random number table to generate a random list.

Limitations

- The sample may still not be representative; by chance there might be more students in the sample than working adults.
- This will be more time consuming than opportunity sampling.

Stratified sample: different sub-groups (strata) within the population are identified and a sample is randomly selected from each. Each sub-group is thus represented proportionately. For example, if the target population includes everyone in a college and there are 1,000 students and 300 members of staff, then the sample should have ten students for every three members of staff.

Limitations

- It is sometimes difficult to identify the sub-groups.
- It can be time-consuming and complicated.
- Simply by chance, all the key characteristics of the target population may not be identified or represented in the sample.

Systematic sample: every 'nth' member of the target population is chosen, e.g. every third student on all of a school's class registers.

Limitations

- The sample may not be representative.
- Compared with random sampling, it may not be quite as unbiased because the researcher has some control over the selection process.

> **Examiner tip**
> Although students are generally able to suggest a method of obtaining a random sample, problems arise when it comes to stating what is meant by a random sample. A random sample does not mean going up to people 'at random'.

After studying this topic, you should be able to:

- understand the concepts of probability and significance levels
- know how to interpret levels of significance
- know how to read statistical tables
- formulate hypotheses and make decisions as to the type of hypothesis required
- understand the difference between Type I and Type II errors
- interpret correlation coefficients and scattergrams of positive, negative and zero correlations
- outline and evaluate different sampling techniques with particular reference to generalisation

Summary

Statistical tests

Summary specification content

The use of parametric and non-parametric tests. Statistical tests of difference: the sign test; Wilcoxon signed ranks test; Mann–Whitney; related t-test (repeated measures) and independent t-test. Statistical tests of association: Spearman's rank order correlation; Pearson's product moment correlation; the Chi-square test. Factors affecting the choice of statistical test, including levels of measurement and type of experimental design. Criteria for parametric testing: interval data, normal distribution and homogeneity of variance.

You will not be required to compute a statistical test in the exam but you will be expected to know which test is appropriate in given circumstances and why. You could also be asked to interpret test statistics by reading a table of critical values and drawing conclusions.

Use of parametric and non-parametric tests

Parametric tests make certain assumptions about the parameters of the population (e.g. mean or standard deviation) from which the sample is drawn. Parametric tests are:

- **Powerful**. They are sensitive to the features of the data collected, so more likely to detect statistically significant effects.
- **Comprehensive**. They use all the information available (they look at the size of differences and the values involved, not just the order of sizes).
- **Robust**. There are certain assumptions underlying their use, but it is possible to do a parametric test on data which do not fit the assumptions precisely.

Non-parametric tests do not require the same assumptions about the population from which the sample is drawn and are:

- Simpler and quicker to compute than parametric tests.
- Capable of being used more widely.
- Not as powerful as parametric tests — they only use the rank order of the scores.
- In need of a higher number of scores/participants in order to match the power of parametric tests.

Statistical tests calculate the probability of chance in a set of findings produced by a piece of research. Sometimes the research is concerned with a **difference** between two conditions and at other times it seeks to determine if there is an **association** or **correlation** between two sets of scores.

Statistical tests of difference

Tests to be used on a related design only:

- **Sign test** or binomial sign test: this converts raw data into categories ('+', '–' and '0'). There is no information about the size of the differences only the **direction** of the differences. The sign test is a **non-parametric** test.

Knowledge check 32

Are parametric tests more likely or less likely to result in a Type II error than non-parametric tests?

Examiner tip

To help you remember the strengths of parametric tests, think of a mnemonic technique e.g. **r**eally **c**ool **p**roduct: robust, comprehensive and powerful.

- **Wilcoxon signed ranks test**: this looks at the differences between related values of pairs and **ranks** these. It uses more information than the sign test so is more sensitive to the differences in the data. The Wilcoxon test is also a **non-parametric** test.
- **Related t-test**: this is a **parametric** test and uses all the information available. It is the most powerful of the three.

Tests to be used on an unrelated design only:
- **Mann–Whitney**: this is the equivalent of the Wilcoxon test. Ranked scores are used rather than actual scores. It is **non-parametric**.
- **Independent t-test:** this is the equivalent of the related t-test. It is **parametric** and more powerful than the Mann–Whitney test.

Statistical tests of association

Spearman's rank order correlation: this measures the **strength** of a relationship between pairs of related values. It uses **ranked** values not actual values. It can also assess the **significance** of the association. It is **non-parametric**.

Pearson's product moment correlation: this test measures the *strength* of a relationship between pairs of related values and can only be used with data that have been measured on an interval scale. It is **parametric.**

The **chi-squared** test: this assesses the **association** between two variables. Data are collected in the form of frequencies and placed in a (contingency) table of any number of rows and columns. Entries in each 'cell' of the table are **discrete**. The test is **non-parametric** and can be used as a test of **difference** for an unrelated design (equivalent to the sign test).

Factors affecting the choice of a statistical test

Levels of measurement

Data can be measured at different levels of detail:
- **Nominal level**: data are simply **categorised** and can be counted (**frequency** data), e.g. 10 smokers and 25 non-smokers. The categories are discrete — smoker or non-smoker.
- **Ordinal level**: data are **ordered** but intervals between each value are unequal, e.g. the rank ordering of finalists in a talent show. This level of measurement should be used when research produces data based on estimates.
- **Interval data**: these are not only ordered but all the intervals between the values are equal, e.g. measurement of temperature. When an interval scale starts from zero it is called a **ratio** scale, e.g. time.

Type of experimental design

When selecting a test of **difference**, you have to consider if the design used to produce the two sets of scores is a related design, i.e. repeated/related measures design, matched pairs design, or an **unrelated design** such as independent groups design. Different designs require different tests.

Examiner tip
If the researcher tests the same group of people (related design) in a 'before and after study', for example a course of treatment, and the data collected is recorded as verbal responses such as feel 'better', 'worse', 'same', then the only suitable test is the sign test. The data can be categorised and responses converted to '+', '−' and '0' difference.

Examiner tip
You have probably noticed that the tests have not been presented in random order within the two design categories but in order of how powerful they are. Notice also that the power of each test depends upon the data/scores it requires for its use.

Knowledge check 33
What is meant by 'discrete' data/scores?

Examiner tip
If asked to identify and justify the level of measurement in a study, the statement 'the data is ordinal' is rarely correct. If you mean you cannot be sure that the data is from a safe numerical scale (equal intervals) e.g. scores in a memory test, say so. The final decision should be to 'treat the data as ordinal'.

Examiner tip

'Homogeneity' means similarity. The variance is a measure of dispersion. The standard deviations can be 'eyeballed' in the exam to check they are similar, as the standard deviation squared gives you the variance.

Criteria for a parametric test

Parametric tests require:
- Data of **interval** status.
- Sample data that are drawn from a **normal distribution**. For small samples, such an assumption can be made on the basis of information from theory or past research. For larger samples, it may be possible to sketch both sample distributions to see if they look normal (bell-shaped).
- Samples must have similar variances (**homogeneity of variance**). The standard deviations can be studied to see if they are similar (or an F-test can be used).

Examiner tip

Justifying the choice for a statistical test is important. You must learn the table. Use a mnemonic technique to help you recall it in the exam. When justifying your choice, go through each of the three points and apply these to the stem material (the description of the study).

Evaluation

Parametric tests are robust: even marked departures from the basic assumptions (other than interval data) can be tolerated except where the sample size and variance are different or the sample is small.

Choosing a statistical test

Three questions need to be asked:
(1) Is a test of **difference** or **relationship/association** required?
(2) What type of **design** has been used, related or unrelated?
(3) What level of measurement has been used? This determines whether or not a parametric test can be used.

	Tests of difference		Tests of relationship
	Independent design	**Related design (repeated or matched)**	**Related design**
Nominal data	Chi-squared test	Sign test	Chi-squared test
Ordinal data	Mann–Whitney test	Wilcoxon signed ranks test	Spearman's rank order correlation
Interval data	Independent t-test	Related t-test	Pearson's product moment correlation

Summary

After studying this topic, you should be able to:
- evaluate parametric and non-parametric tests
- understand the criteria for the use of parametric tests
- correctly select a statistical test to analyse the data collected
- justify your choice of the statistical test

AQA(B) A2 Psychology

Issues in research

Summary specification content

Strengths and limitations of different methods of research. Strengths and limitations of qualitative and quantitative data. Reliability and validity applied generally across all methods of investigation. Ways of assessing reliability, including test-retest and inter-observer. Ways of assessing validity including face validity and concurrent validity. Critical understanding of the importance of ethical considerations within the social and cultural environment. Ethical considerations in the design and conduct of psychological studies and within psychology as a whole.

You should be familiar with the different methods of research, having covered these on the AS course and having had direct practical experience in your studies. Only a brief summary of strengths and limitations is given here. You should also have had experience of the application of ethical considerations in the design and conduct of psychological studies.

Strengths and limitations of different methods of research

Experiment

Strengths of the experimental method

- It can establish cause and effect between the independent variable (IV) and dependent variable (DV).
- It is the most scientific of all the methods. Controlled procedures and objective measures mean that replication is possible and reliability can be checked.

Limitations of the experimental method

- Experiments often lack ecological validity due to controlled settings.
- There can be problems with demand characteristics: participants often look for clues as to expected behaviour.

Questionnaires

Strengths of the questionnaire method

- Large amounts of data can be collected relatively quickly.
- Questionnaires using closed questions can be replicated quite easily.
- Open-ended questions can provide rich and detailed information.

Limitations of the questionnaire method

- Social desirability may influence responses.
- Closed questions in particular are susceptible to response set.
- They rely on self-report data which may be biased.

Knowledge check 34

What feature of the laboratory experimental method allows the researcher to make causal statements about behaviour?

Examiner tip

Remember that there are three types of experiment you are required to know (field, laboratory, quasi), all of which have different strengths and limitations. Bear this in mind in answer to questions on the experimental method.

Interviews

Strengths of the interview method
- Large amounts of data can be gathered.
- It provides access to information not easily available by other methods.

Limitations of the interview method
- It relies on self-report, which can be subjective.
- It is difficult to establish cause and effect links.
- With limited choice answers, information may be excluded.
- Open questions may be difficult to summarise.

Correlation studies

Examiner tip
Strictly speaking a 'correlation' is a method of data analysis and not a type of study. Think of a 'correlational study' as an investigation using correlational analysis. The terms independent variable and dependent variable are not used. This is because there is no direct manipulation of variables as in an experiment.

Strengths of correlation studies
- Correlations show a relationship between two variables.
- Correlations enable predictions about increase/decrease in one variable over another.
- They are useful where experimental manipulation would be unethical.

Limitations of correlation studies
- Correlations cannot show cause and effect.
- Any relationship may be due to some other unknown variable.

Observational studies

Examiner tip
Remember that some observations take place in a laboratory and so will not be high in ecological validity. If you refer to ecological validity as a strength, check that the point applies to the question and always qualify 'ecological validity'.

Strengths of the observational method
- It is high in ecological validity.
- It is useful where experimental manipulation would be unethical.

Limitations of the observational method
- The observer cannot infer cause and effect (unless part of an experiment).
- It is prone to observer bias.
- It is difficult to replicate.
- If participants know that they are being watched, they may change their behaviour. If they do not know, then this raises additional ethical problems.

Content analysis

Strengths of content analysis
- There are few ethical issues because participants are not directly involved.
- It allows researchers to study a wide range of material.

Limitations of content analysis

- Behaviour is being studied out of context, so it could be misinterpreted.
- Categories are decided in advance and are based on the researcher's expectations.
- Qualitative content analyses are open to interpretation.

Case studies

Strengths of the case study method

- The data produced are rich in detail.
- It has high validity because it relates to real life.
- A single case can be used to challenge a theory.
- It may be the only way to study unusual or rare behaviour.

Limitations of the case study method

- Results cannot be generalised.
- It often involves retrospective data, which may be unreliable.
- The close relationship between researcher and participant may introduce bias.
- Cause and effect are difficult to establish.
- It is not based on a rigorous methodology, so replication is not possible.

Strengths and limitations of qualitative and quantitative data

Qualitative data are non-numerical, descriptive data represented in words rather than numbers. They generally represent the thoughts and feelings that a person has, e.g. the **quality** of an experience or some aspect of behaviour.

Quantitative data are numerical and represent **how much** there is of something, e.g. the score in a memory test.

Qualitative data can be converted into quantitative data, e.g. by categorising responses in an interview and calculating frequencies of certain types of response.

Strengths of qualitative data

- They can be useful in generating new theories.
- They focus on issues that are meaningful to the participant — in other words, they have high face validity.
- They are richer and more detailed — they describe rather than numerically score behaviour.
- Behaviour can be studied in context.

Examiner tip
Answers on the strengths of qualitative data often state little other than 'rich and detailed information'. However, quantitative data can also be 'rich and detailed'. Always qualify your answer — one way of doing this is to make comparisons with quantitative data. Providing contrast to bring out the strength is particularly effective given that much research in psychology collects quantitative data.

Limitations of qualitative data
- They are difficult to replicate.
- Data analysis is difficult.
- It is difficult to establish cause and effect links.
- They are subjective and low in reliability.

Strengths of quantitative data
- They can be easily summarised into graphs or statistics.
- They are easy to replicate.
- They are objective data, so easier to analyse.

Limitations of quantitative data
- They have low ecological validity.
- They are less meaningful than qualitative data.

Reliability and validity applied generally across all methods of investigation

Reliability refers to whether a finding can be repeated and whether a method of measurement produces consistent results over varying time and place. This applies to all methods of investigation, e.g. an experiment, questionnaire, observational procedure, psychometric test etc.

Validity refers to whether a test, measurement or experimental manipulation is doing what was originally intended. This also applies to all methods of investigation.

Types of reliability and ways of assessing these

Within an experiment or research in general, reliability can be assessed through **replication**.

Inter-observer/rater reliability should be assessed where measuring involves several observers or 'raters', such as in observations or interviews. Reliability can be assessed by observers checking their observations for agreement. There should be a **strong positive correlation**.

Intra-observer/rater reliability is assessed when the same observer makes repeated observations which are checked against each other for agreement.

Internal reliability is the extent to which a measure is consistent within itself. It can be checked by the **split-half method**, whereby the results of half the items on the test are correlated with the results from the other half. **Item analysis** is another way to check for the internal reliability of a questionnaire/test.

External reliability is the extent to which a measure is consistent from one use to another. It can be checked by **test-retest**. This involves correlating the results of a measure gained on one occasion with those gained on a later occasion.

Equivalent/parallel forms avoid time delay; two equivalent or similar tests are given and the results are correlated.

Examiner tip

'Inter' means 'between' and 'intra' means 'within'. So in inter-observer reliability, at least two people/observers are involved and their scores are compared with one another or 'between' themselves for agreement. In intra-observer reliability, only one person/rater is involved and scores are compared 'within' that person alone to check for agreement.

Knowledge check 35

Why must the test-retest method always build in some time delay between the two occasions of testing?

Types of validity and ways of assessing these

External validity refers to whether the results can be generalised when applied to different settings (**ecological validity**), times or groups of participants.

Internal validity refers to whether the results of the study were really due to the experimental manipulation.

Face/content validity — examining the content of a test to see if it looks as if it is measuring what it is supposed to be measuring.

Construct validity — the extent to which a test measures the trait or theoretical construct that it is designed to measure.

Criterion validity — whether a test gives a predictable result when used with a group whose results might be anticipated (a criterion group). For example, a group of athletes should score highly on a test of coordination.

Concurrent validity — involves correlating results on a test with results on an already established test of the same measure. If the new test is valid, a strong positive correlation should be found.

Predictive validity — where scores on a test correlate with some measure of future behaviour, e.g. scores on a job selection test should show a strong positive correlation with future job performance.

Critical understanding of the importance of ethical considerations within the social and cultural environment

Scientific research has greatly improved the quality of life for many people. However, research is funded by society, for the benefit of society and it is the duty of all scientists to consider ethical issues associated with the research, its findings and implications within the broader context of the social and cultural environment. Scientists have ethical codes based on humanistic, moral and religious beliefs which must take account of the different values and beliefs within a multi-cultural and multi-ethnic society. The process of **peer review** plays an important role in ensuring integrity and assessing the value of research.

Ethical considerations in the design and conduct of psychological studies and within psychology as a whole

Code of ethics as specified by the British Psychological Society

The Code of Ethics and Conduct (2006) set out by the British Psychological Society (BPS) is designed to:

- protect participants, patients and clients
- maintain professional standards
- provide a framework and guide decisions about appropriate conduct

Examiner tip

It is important to give all the details about assessing reliability or validity, e.g. type of reliability/validity, source of the data, how it is collected and statistical analysis. Make sure that you know the types of reliability and validity listed explicitly in the specification.

Applying the code of ethics in research

The code contains four headings: Respect, Competence, Responsibility and Integrity, each of which has certain specifications.

(1) Respect — the researcher should respect individuals and avoid unfairness and prejudice. In addition:

- **Confidentiality**: information about participants should not be made available to others without their informed consent.
- **Informed consent**: participants must know what they are consenting to.
- **Privacy**: participants' privacy should be respected at all times.
- **Deception**: this should be avoided and the participant informed as soon as possible.
- **Right to withdraw**: participants can withdraw themselves or their data at any time.

(2) Competence — only qualified psychologists should give advice.

(3) Responsibility — researchers have a responsibility to their participants, in terms of:

- **Protection from harm**: researchers should ensure the psychological well-being and physical health of their participants.
- **Debriefing**: participants should be told the details of the research and its purpose after the investigation.

(4) Integrity — psychologists should be honest and maintain professional boundaries.

Examiner tip

If application of an ethical issue is required, ensure you identify the ethical issue, e.g. protection from harm, and explain in what way it presents as an ethical issue. It may also be useful to say how the issue might be addressed.

Questions & Answers

The examination

The Unit 4 examination is 2 hours long and you have to answer questions from three sections: one on Approaches in Psychology, one on Debates in Psychology and one on Methods in Psychology. Each section carries 20 marks so you should allow 40 minutes for each section in the examination. The Approaches and Debates questions are structured, which means that there are several sub-sections to each question. The first sub-sections are short-answer questions usually worth 2, 3 or 4 marks. These are followed by a final sub-section that requires extended writing for 12 marks. The Methods in Psychology section is more heavily structured than the other sections, consisting of lots of sub-sections requiring short answers.

Short-answer questions

- Commands like 'identify', 'state', 'name', 'suggest' and 'give' require the very briefest of answers.
- Commands like 'outline' and 'describe' require straightforward description.
- Commands like 'explain' and 'distinguish' require some analysis or elaboration of concepts. In the case of 'distinguish' you need to explain the difference/s between two things.
- The command 'briefly discuss' requires some description and some evaluation or criticism and is usually worth 4 or 5 marks.
- If asked to 'describe a study' for 4 marks, you should refer explicitly to the aim, method, results and conclusion.

Examples of short-answer questions

- Identify **two** assumptions of the cognitive approach.
- Explain what psychodynamic psychologists mean by *unconscious mental processes*.
- Give **two** limitations of the behaviourist approach.
- State what is meant by *an eclectic approach*.
- Outline **two** strengths of idiographic research.
- Describe **one** study in which the genetic basis of behaviour was investigated.
- Briefly discuss **one** way of assessing the reliability of a psychological measure.
- Distinguish between hard and soft determinism.

Long-answer questions

These are worth 12 marks. A typical 12-mark question would ask you to 'describe and evaluate' a theory, an explanation or some research. In 12-mark questions, 4 marks are for description and knowledge and 8 are for evaluation/analysis/application/comparison. In the evaluation, you should present strengths and limitations. If relevant, you should support what you say with reference to evidence and explain how this relates to the topic. You can also get evaluation marks by comparing; for example by introducing an opposing theory to illustrate the limitations of the theory you are discussing. You should aim to spend plenty of time on this sub-section of the question in the examination.

Some 12-mark questions ask you to 'refer to topics in psychology in your answers'. 'Topics' means content areas of the specification that you have covered over the AS and A2 years; for example, gender, forensic psychology, schizophrenia etc.

In the 12-mark questions you will be assessed on your ability to communicate. You should therefore make sure that your answer is properly structured into sentences and paragraphs and pay attention to your spelling. If a 12-mark question asks you to 'refer to evidence' or 'refer to another approach', there will be a limit to the number of marks that you will be awarded if you do not comply with that instruction.

Mark schemes for 12-mark questions are banded into 'very good', 'good', 'average to weak' and 'poor', which means that the examiner will not only consider each individual point that you make, but will also make a general assessment of the answer as a whole. Students who show good knowledge and make plenty of evaluation points but do not present a well-argued response, will sometimes be awarded a lower mark than they might have been given because the answer as a whole is better suited to the 'good' band than to the 'very good' band.

Scenario questions

In some questions, you must use your knowledge by applying what you have learned about psychology to a novel situation. For example, a question might include a scenario about a person who suffers from low self-esteem. In this case, you might be required to use your knowledge of Rogers (a humanistic psychologist) to explain the person's experience. You could describe how Rogers suggested that low self-esteem occurs as a result of a discrepancy (incongruence) between our perceived self and the way we would like to be (our ideal self). This sort of question tests your application of knowledge.

Assessment of practical psychology and research methods

In Unit 4, your knowledge of practical psychology and research methods will be tested in the Methods section and also within the context of the Approaches and Debates questions. The Methods section will start with a description of a psychological study. This will be followed by a number of short-answer questions about different aspects of the study. There may also be questions where you are expected to make suggestions for alterations or improvements to the study that has been described, or to design a further study. This is testing your practical experience of psychological research or 'how science works'. For this reason, it is important that you have had practical experience of designing and implementing psychological research in your class activities. You will be expected to know about how to use and interpret inferential statistical tests, but you will not be expected to calculate an inferential test in an examination. It is important that you are familiar with all the tests, their conditions of use and how to use statistical tables.

Synopticity

At A2 you are expected to be able to demonstrate an understanding of psychology as a whole. You will notice that questions on the Unit 4 paper often ask you to 'refer to at **least one** topic' in your answer. This is asking you to relate your knowledge of the various topic areas you have studied at AS and A2 (e.g. memory, social influence, anxiety disorders, stress, substance abuse) to your understanding of the broader approaches, debates and methods in psychology. This is your chance to present a unique and considered response, which integrates knowledge of specific topics and more general psychological ideas and issues. A word of warning: be careful to remain focused on the question here and not to deviate into a discussion confined to the topic itself.

Assessment objectives

Examination boards use the term assessment objective (AO) to refer to the different types of skills a student might be expected to demonstrate in examinations. Your teacher might have told you about AO1, AO2 and AO3 skills:

- AO1 refers to knowledge and understanding.
- AO2 refers to analysis and evaluation and the application of knowledge to novel situations.
- AO3 refers to knowledge and understanding of research methods and practical psychology.

You should not worry too much about these different skills in the examination. In most cases the wording of the question will lead you to demonstrate the necessary skills. Only the following two types of question require you to think about AO skills:

- 'Describe and evaluate', 'discuss' or 'compare' for 12 marks. Whatever the wording of the 12-mark question, 4 marks are for description (AO1) and 8 marks are for evaluation, analysis and application (AO2). In a 12-mark question you should aim to present an appropriate balance of description and evaluation/analysis/application.
- 'Briefly discuss' for 3, 4 or 5 marks. Here there would normally be 1 or 2 marks for description (AO1) and 2 or 3 marks for evaluation, analysis and application (AO2).

Sample questions and answers

In this section of the guide, there are six questions — two on each section of the unit. Each question is worth 20 marks. You should allow 30 minutes when answering a question.

The section is structured as follows:

- sample questions in the style in which they appear on the Unit 4 examination paper
- analysis of each question, explaining what is expected in each sub-section of the question
- example student responses at the C/D-grade level (student A) — these have been selected to illustrate particular strengths and limitations
- example student responses at the A-grade level (student B) — such answers demonstrate thorough knowledge, a good understanding and an ability to analyse the data and issues raised in the questions

Examiners' comments

All student responses are followed by examiners' comments. These are preceded by the icon @. They indicate where credit is due and, in the weaker answer, they also point out areas for improvement, specific problems and common errors such as poor time management, lack of clarity, weak or non-existent development, irrelevance, misinterpretation of the question and mistaken meanings of terms. The comments also indicate how each example answer might be marked in an actual exam.

Question 1 Approaches in psychology (I)

(a) Identify and explain one way in which psychologists have investigated the genetic basis of behaviour. (4 marks)

ⓔ This question is assessing your knowledge of how science and practical psychology work by asking you how psychologists go about investigating something as complex as the genetic basis of behaviour. Although you will not have had hands-on experience of such research yourself, you are expected to explain the methodology of others' experimental work. To answer this question you need to think of one way, most likely twin studies, and go through the rationale of the method. Make sure that you tell the examiner clearly how the rationale of your chosen method informs about the genetic basis of behaviour. If you feel that it would help, give an example of behaviour. Avoid describing a study and listing several ways.

(b) Sadie is a disruptive 6-year-old girl. Her teacher is seeking help from an educational psychologist to make Sadie behave in class. The psychologist recommends a therapy based on the principles of operant conditioning.

(i) Outline what is meant by *operant conditioning*. (2 marks)

(ii) Explain how operant conditioning could be applied to change Sadie's behaviour. (2 marks)

ⓔ This question has been split into two parts, making it easier for you to follow both requirements. For (i) you need to state clearly what is meant by the term. To get both marks, your outline needs to be both clear and accurate. The second part (ii) is testing your understanding of how operant conditioning can be applied. Make sure that you apply your answer to Sadie's behaviour and that you provide an explanation.

(c) Discuss the psychodynamic approach. Refer to at least one other approach in your answer. (12 marks)

ⓔ This part requires an extended answer and you will be assessed on the quality of your written communication as well as the psychological content. In this question, the bulk of the marks are for discussion, so focus on analysis, application and evaluation. One third of the marks is reserved for knowledge and understanding, which can include an outline of the approach. It is a good idea to use specialist terminology as this will also gain marks, if relevant. Notice that you are asked to refer to at least one other approach. This gives you the opportunity to make comparisons and should help you when evaluating and analysing the psychodynamic approach. Finally, be aware that if you fail to refer to another approach, then you will not be able to get more than 8 marks, however good your answer.

Student A

(a) Psychologists have used twin studies to investigate the genetic basis of behaviour **a**. Monozygotic twins are identical — they have the same genes and they can be compared with DZ twins, who are not identical **b**, to see if MZ twins are more alike **c**. They can also use adoption studies **d**.

ⓔ **2/4 marks awarded. a** The student has correctly identified one way, which gains a mark. **b** Another mark is given for the comparison between identical twins and non-identical twins. **c** This point, however, should be analysed and developed to say how the results of such comparisons can be interpreted. **d** Although adoption studies are also used, only one way was required so no credit was given for this.

> **(b) (i)** Operant conditioning was studied by Skinner. He placed rats in a box. If the rat pressed a lever it got some food as a reward. This is operant conditioning **a**.

🅔 **1/2 marks awarded. a** There is some knowledge of operant conditioning demonstrated by the example of reward as a consequence of the response. However, the student is not able to analyse or convey the principles of operant conditioning in the explanation. Ideally, the concept of positive reinforcement should have been noted.

> **(ii)** Sadie could be given a reward, such as a sweet, every time she behaves well **b**. She should be ignored when she is disruptive and then the behaviour will stop **c**.

🅔 **1/2 marks awarded. b** This answer also conveys a hint of understanding in the idea that there should be a positive consequence for good behaviour. A sweet is a sensible suggestion for a six-year-old, showing that the student is applying the answer to Sadie. **c** The point about ignoring bad behaviour is relevant. However, this answer lacks explanation — it is only providing an outline of the application of operant conditioning to Sadie's behaviour. This part gets 1 mark for a good outline, but some attempt at an explanation of why ignoring behaviour causes extinction or why a sweet would change Sadie's behaviour would push it up to the full 2 marks.

> **(c)** Freud developed his theory in Austria in the late nineteenth century. He believed that childhood experiences had a huge impact on later adult behaviour **b**. This belief is now very much accepted but in Freud's time, it was not really thought that childhood was important.
>
> Freud also set out the different parts of the mind. These are the unconscious, subconscious and conscious **a c**. He believed that most of our mental processes occur in the unconscious and that we did not really know what is happening in our mind. Also, we do not always understand the reasons for our behaviour. The problem with this assumption is that you can't prove it **f**.
>
> Freud also put forward the three parts of the personality, the id, ego and superego. He said that the child was born with the id only and that the ego and superego developed later on in childhood **d**. The ego was said to be responsible for defence mechanisms such as repression, where anxieties are thought to be repressed in the unconscious. This protects the person **e**. He supported this with his case studies like Little Hans and Anna O. Anna O had a paralysed arm because of unconscious fears which had become repressed. But once these fears had become clear through therapy, her paralysis was cured. The problem with case studies like this is that the evidence is subjective. Freud interpreted the case studies so as to fit his theories — he was able to explain but not predict **g**. This means that he did not use a scientific approach, unlike the Behaviourists, who always used objective measurements such as how much saliva a dog produced to measure learning **h**. The problem, though, with the behaviourist approach is that they use animals but humans are more complicated than animals **i**.

One strength of Freud's theory is that it is useful in therapy. This is called psychoanalysis and has been applied to many examples such as anxiety, trying to gain insight into what is unconsciously causing the symptoms of obsessive-compulsive disorder. Techniques like free association can be used to find the unconscious fear **j**. This makes it similar to the behaviourist approach that has also produced practical applications **k**.

In summary, the psychodynamic approach is broad and has similarities and differences with the behaviourist approach. Its main limitation is that it is not really scientific.

ⓔ **7/12 marks awarded (AO1 = 4, AO2 = 3). a** This answer shows good knowledge and understanding of the psychodynamic approach. It is generally accurate ('preconscious' should be used rather than 'subconscious') and is logically structured. AO1 credit can be awarded for each of the following points: **b** the impact of childhood on adult behaviour; **c** the different parts of the mind; **d** the three parts of personality and the **e** elaboration given on the ego and function of defence mechanisms. **f** Efforts at analysis and evaluation were less successful because of lack of elaboration. AO2 credit was almost gained for the reference to lack of proof for the processes of the unconscious but, unfortunately, this point was not explained. Simply stating that the problem is that you 'can't prove it' is not enough. **g** AO2 credit was awarded for the point that the methodology was unscientific; this was clearly elaborated by 'he was able to explain but not predict'. **h** The comparison with the behaviourist approach satisfied the requirement of the question to make reference to another approach, and was relevant and sufficiently developed to gain credit. The reference to objective measurement was particularly successful. **i** The problem of the use of animals in the behaviourist approach is not relevant to the question so cannot gain credit. Straight evaluation of the 'other approach' is a common failing in exam questions of this kind. Had some evaluative comparison been made with the psychodynamic approach, then credit could have been given. **j** The application to therapy is clear and well developed as an evaluative point so also can gain credit. **k** However, simply stating that this is a point of similarity with the behaviourist approach is not creditworthy.

This is not a top band answer but a low level second band response. Its strengths lie in knowledge and understanding rather than analysis and evaluation.

Total for this question: 11 out of 20 marks — grade D.

Student B

(a) Psychologists have used twin studies to investigate the genetic basis of behaviour **a**. If one identical twin (MZ) has a particular characteristic which is genetic then so should the other twin as they share the same genes. There should be a 100% concordance rate. DZ twins or non-identical twins **b** should show a much lower concordance rate, nearer 50%, as they only share half their genes **c**. In such comparisons, genes are effectively 'manipulated' and the environment held constant, allowing psychologists to investigate the genetic basis of behaviour **d**.

ⓔ **4/4 marks awarded. a** The student has correctly identified one way, which gains a mark. **b** Another mark is given for the comparison between identical twins and non-identical twins. **c** The accurate reference to the two sets of concordance rates shows good understanding and is relevant to the explanation, so is worth another mark. It is good practice to use specialist terminology wherever possible (such as 'concordance rate'). **d** The final sentence completes the explanation, informing the examiner that the student really does understands the rationale of such studies and 'how science works'.

(b) (i) Operant conditioning is learning through the consequences of behaviour; for example, reinforcement or punishment. If the behaviour is followed by positive or negative reinforcement, then this increases the probability of the response being repeated **a**. Punishment means that the behaviour is unlikely to be repeated.

ⓔ **2/2 marks awarded. a** The answer offers a clear and accurate outline of operant conditioning and refers correctly to the key terms: 'reinforcement', 'consequences of behaviour', 'the response being repeated'. All this shows a good understanding of the principles of operant conditioning and is enough for the full 2 marks.

(ii) Sadie could be given something she wants, like a gold star, every time she behaves well. This would act as positive reinforcement and would 'stamp in' the response (good behaviour), meaning that it would be repeated **a**. Sadie is probably getting attention when she is disruptive — this is also a form of positive reinforcement so the teacher must ignore her when she is being disruptive. A response that is ignored (has no consequence) eventually dies out, so gold stars for good behaviour replace attention for bad behaviour **b**.

ⓔ **2/2 marks awarded. a** The reference to the 'good behaviour' being repeated is a basic point but crucial to the explanation and is worth 1 mark. **b** This is an excellent response, fully explaining how Sadie's behaviour could be 'manipulated'. The answer shows a sound and accurate understanding of how operant conditioning could be applied to replace one type of desired consequence (attention) with another (gold star). Notice that there are only 2 marks available here so you need to be sensible as to how much to write. There is still more that you could write about, for example, successive approximation, but for 2 marks there is sufficient.

(c) The psychodynamic approach was first established by Freud. His theory in fact consisted of several mini-theories. One theory was that the unconscious mind is the major cause of behaviour **b**. Freud believed that the unconscious contains repressed innate instincts and desires, fears, anxieties and memories. However, repressed material does not remain dormant in the unconscious but is expressed in behaviour. For example, if a parent represses hostile feelings towards their child, an aspect of their behaviour might be to shower the child with presents **c**.

Another theory was his outline of the structure of the mind. The id is based on the pleasure principle and is present at birth. The ego emerges in early infancy and is based on the reality principle. Whereas the id is unconscious, the ego, being based on reality, is mainly conscious. Finally the superego develops and is based on the morality principle. The three parts of personality are in constant conflict, as the rational ego and moral superego try to contain the id impulses. This is why ego defence mechanisms are sometimes employed to keep the

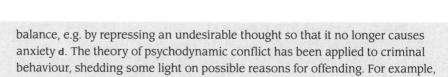

balance, e.g. by repressing an undesirable thought so that it no longer causes anxiety **d**. The theory of psychodynamic conflict has been applied to criminal behaviour, shedding some light on possible reasons for offending. For example, crime arises from an under-developed superego **a e**.

The final aspect of Freud's theory was that of psychosexual development. Freud believed that we all pass through the same stages of psychosexual development in the same order; a deterministic attitude **f**. One of his boldest claims was that of childhood sexuality, another that adult behaviour is affected by childhood experiences and in particular their relationship with parents. Freud uses psychosexual stages to explain all aspects of childhood development and adult personality **g**. As an example, a fixation at the anal stage might lead to a personality centred on either tidiness or messiness **h**. However, it could be argued that this focus on childhood sexuality is inappropriate and overstated. Piaget, who represents the cognitive approach, focused far more on what mental processes children and adults were capable of, as opposed to Freud's view of constant conflict and unconscious repression of unacceptable urges (e.g. Oedipus conflict) **i**.

Freud developed his theories through the use of case studies. He illustrated the concept of castration anxiety using the case study of little Hans — explaining Hans' fear of horses and being bitten by one as fear of castration by his father. However interesting this interpretation might be, the problem is that you cannot generalise from one case study or even a few case studies to all children. The accuracy of Freud's assessment is also questionable. He was selective in the information he used; for example, he omitted to include the fact that Hans' mother threatened Hans with castration. In fact, Freud did not work directly with Hans but corresponded with his father. Clearly his techniques were not objective and were open to bias **j**.

Erikson modified Freud's theory and formed the psychosocial theory in place of Freud's psychosexual theory. His theory emphasised the role of social factors in the development of personality. Like Freud, he referred to crises at each of his eight stages. Totally different approaches to development are offered by the humanistic psychologists. Their view of constant striving for self-actualisation is more optimistic than Freud's belief that humans are in constant conflict and destructive by nature **k**. In a way, the biological approach to development overlaps with the psychodynamic approach, as it also focuses on instincts and inherited tendencies **l**.

The psychodynamic approach does have its critics. The main criticism is that it is irrefutable and theoretically unscientific. Freud has an answer for any outcome. For example, by applying the defence mechanism of reaction formation, he can explain the opposite of what might logically be predicted by the theory. This can be compared with the behaviourist approach, which is based on objective, observable behaviour and theories which lead to predictions of behaviour **m**. However, the psychodynamic approach has been profoundly influential, with phrases such as 'fixation' and 'defence mechanism' finding their way into popular speech. Although the case studies of Freud do not allow for generalisations, one defence of the approach is that studying individual cases and attempting really to understand and describe behaviour is also an aim of science. Perhaps Freud is more of a scientist than experimental psychologists such as the Behaviourists, who study people as objects responding to the environment **n**.

(e) 12/12 marks awarded **(AO1 = 4, AO2 = 8).** **a** Two immediate observations are the breadth of information included and the coherence of the discussion. Clearly the student has come into the exam well informed and well prepared to deliver such an outstanding discussion. The student sets the scene effectively, bringing in the key points about the approach in a logical order: **b** the reference to the unconscious mind, **c** repression and an example to illustrate, **d** also the structure of the mind and psychodynamic conflict **e** (the application to crime is correct and relevant to the discussion, earning AO2 credit). All these points earn AO1 credit. **f** There are, in fact, several more points within the answer that could earn AO1 credit should this be required, e.g. the psychosexual stages of development. **g** You may notice that the student does not actually outline these stages of development, which leaves more time for the discussion. This is a good strategy, **h** though in this case the example of fixation at the anal stage is not set in context. **i** However, linking into the cognitive approach and Piaget allows for comparison and is relevant to the argument — a creditworthy AO2 point. **j** The limitations of the methodology which follow also gain AO2 credit. **k** Notice that, having given some consideration to methodology, the student goes on to discuss theoretical issues. The reference to Erikson gives breadth to the approach (and would have earned AO1 credit if needed) and leads logically into an evaluative comparison with the humanistic approach, providing further AO2 credit. **l** The reference to the biological approach shows knowledge and understanding and is an interesting observation, but does not add to the discussion. **m** However, comparison with the behaviourist approach is effectively done, so provides AO2 credit. **n** Finally, to give a really rounded discussion, mentioning the strengths of the approach earns AO2 credit.

This is a very good answer, focused on the question, well-balanced and logical, with well-structured arguments.

Total for this question: 20 out of 20 marks — grade A.

Question 2 Approaches in psychology (II)

(a) Outline two methodological criticisms of the person-centred approach of Rogers and Maslow.

(4 marks)

ⓔ This question is assessing your knowledge of 'how science works' by asking you to take a critical look at how humanistic psychologists go about investigating individual subjective conscious experience. You must take care not to get sidetracked into an outline of how they investigate such experience, but go beyond that and consider the problems with their methods. Also, be careful not to go into problems with their actual theories, although the way one investigates a phenomenon can, of course, have implications for the theory under study. To answer this question you need to identify and outline criticisms around issues such as reliability, validity, falsifiability, sampling, generalisability and objectivity.

(b) Use an example of behaviour to explain what cognitive psychologists mean by mediational processes.

(4 marks)

ⓔ This part is essentially asking you to do two things. First of all, you should state clearly what the term 'mediational processes' means. This term is in the specification under social learning theory but applies equally to the cognitive approach. Any term that appears on the specification can be tested in this manner. The more difficult part is the second requirement of the question and involves conveying the meaning of the term through an example.

(c) Outline and compare the cognitive and behaviourist approaches in psychology.

(12 marks)

ⓔ This section requires an extended answer and you will be assessed on the quality of your written communication as well as the psychological content. In this question, the bulk of the marks are for discussion, so focus on comparing. One third of the marks are reserved for knowledge and understanding, which means you should include an outline of each approach. It is a good idea to use specialist terminology, as this will also gain marks if relevant. When comparing, you can of course point out differences between the two approaches as well as similarities. Think about theoretical and methodological comparisons (theories and research methods). Remember that in these 12-mark questions, you need to show the examiner that you have a really good overview of psychology as a whole, so it is a good idea to link into topic areas, debates or other approaches to broaden your discussion.

Student A

(a) One methodological criticism of the person-centred approach is that it is not scientific **a**. Another is that the approach is culture bound **b** and cannot be easily applied to different societies like people in the third world **e**. This is because it was only tested **d** on people like Lincoln and Eleanor Roosevelt **c**.

ⓔ **1/4 marks awarded. a** The student has correctly identified one way, which gains a mark; this is the reference to the approach not being scientific. There is no elaboration of this point, which would have gained another mark if accurate. **b** The second way — mentioning that the approach is 'culture bound' (presumably concepts and ideas) — is not a methodological criticism. **c** The last sentence is getting closer to answering the question, but **d** the use of the term 'tested' is inappropriate, **e** plus there is no reference to sampling and generalisation of results to link with 'cannot be easily applied to different societies'. There is no convincing evidence in this answer that the student understands 'how science works'.

(b) Mediational processes can be non-conscious or conscious **a** and they are the processes such as attention and memory **c** between the output or the response given and the information received **b d**.

🅔 **2/4 marks awarded. a** The answer is awkwardly expressed and quite brief but does convey a basic understanding of what is meant by 'mediational processes'. There are two creditworthy points here. **b** The first is the idea that these are processes that come between stimulus and response; **c** the second is the inclusion of attention and memory as appropriate examples. These gain AO1 credit for knowledge and understanding. **d** What this answer lacks is the use of an example of how memory and attention mediate between input and output.

(c) The cognitive approach in psychology is an information processing approach. This means that it compares the way the human mind works to the way that computers work. The good thing about such an analogy is that human cognitive processes can be studied scientifically and experiments can be done based on computer models to get a better understanding of how the mind works. For example, models of memory such as the Atkinson Shiffrin model has allowed a lot of experiments to be done on short and long-term memory **b**. Because we are not studying observable behaviour, it helps to have a model to relate to **a**. This is similar to the behaviourist approach, which also uses a scientific approach, e.g. experiments to investigate behaviour. However, the behaviourist approach would not study topics like memory even with the use of computer models because memory is an internal process which cannot be seen **f**.

A disadvantage of the cognitive approach is that it is mechanistic. Humanistic psychologists would say that this approach is dehumanising — people are not computers and have conscious subjective experience and feelings and emotions. The cognitive approach is nomothetic so the results found can be generalised to the whole population. Another good point is that the cognitive approach can be applied, for instance, to atypical behaviour **j**.

Behaviourists believe that only observable behaviour is appropriate to study, as we are unable to see into the mind **c**. Many of the behaviourists' theories of development and behaviour are based on conditioning, e.g. Pavlov and his dog demonstrated classical conditioning. This is where an unconditioned stimulus is paired with a conditioned one (natural stimulus–response link like food and salivation paired with a bell) to create a conditioned response (bell and salivation) **d e**. Operant conditioning is another theory where reinforcement shapes behaviour **a**.

The behaviourist approach has the advantage of being generalisable due to its nomothetic approach, and like the cognitive approach, has many practical applications. However, much of the research is carried out on animals. This method has been criticised due to the belief that humans are qualitatively different **k**.

The cognitive approach is holistic, whereas the behaviourists are reductionist — they reduce behaviour to S–R connections. The cognitive approach looks at what comes in between S–R connections so it is more holistic **g**. A lot of the reaction to the reductionist behaviourist approach came from the Gestalt psychologists, who investigated perception and claimed that 'the whole is more than the sum of its parts' **h**. Occasionally the cognitive approach will use an idiographic case study (e.g. the study of Clive Wearing, whose memory was affected after a virus), unlike the behaviourist approach, which always applies a nomothetic approach. This is a strength of the cognitive approach compared to the behaviourist approach, as it allows richer information to be gathered to support a theory or to provide a basis for further research **i**.

The approaches clearly have similarities and differences with one another but currently the cognitive approach is favoured.

@ **8/12 marks awarded (AO1 = 4, AO2 = 4). a** The reasonably balanced outline of the approaches gains full AO1 credit for each approach. **b** For the cognitive approach, credit was given for reference to information processing and the computer analogy. **c** For the behaviourist approach, credit was given for the focus on observable behaviour and a **d** knowledge and understanding of classical conditioning. **e** Notice the use of terminology here in the references to unconditioned and conditioned stimuli.

f To earn AO2 credit, there must be comparisons between the approaches and 'discussion' or elaboration. There are few examples of this. In the first paragraph, there is a comparison regarding the scientific approach. A similarity is discussed, they both use experiments, but a difference is also recognised — that they have different subject matter. AO2 credit was awarded for these two points. **g** Further AO2 credit was given towards the end of the answer where both approaches were linked to the holism-reductionism debate. **h** The link to Gestalt psychology was appropriate. **i** Finally, the link to nomothetic and idiographic approaches was quite effective, earning AO2 credit. Notice that, for all these comparisons, there was some elaboration or development of the point.

j Several evaluative points did not gain credit as they were not relevant to the question. Paragraph two simply contained a list of evaluative points about the cognitive approach, for which no marks were awarded. **k** Similarly, the evaluation in paragraph four about the behaviourist approach contained a list of points not relevant to the question. Although a similarity is mentioned '… has many practical applications', it was merely stated. This could easily have gained AO2 credit had the comparison been discussed by giving examples of practical applications, such as different treatments etc. The student could also have noted how the two approaches might sometimes overlap to provide more eclectic therapy, such as cognitive-behaviour therapy.

This is a demanding question and it is tempting to take each approach separately, but comparison is necessary throughout, and this student has tried hard to satisfy this requirement.

Total for this question: 11 out of 20 marks — grade D.

(a) The person-centred approach **b** studied the subjective experience of individuals using case studies. One problem in studying people this way is that findings from individuals cannot produce generalised laws of behaviour that apply to other people **e**.

Maslow conducted research **c** on individuals whom he had previously categorised as self-actualisers. The categorisation was based on his definition of a self-actualised person. Categorising people based on one's own definition is subjective and unreliable. A person Maslow categorises as a self-actualiser may not be categorised in the same way by another psychologist. Such a method cannot be regarded as a valid base for his research **f** into the characteristics of self-actualisers **a d**.

ⓔ **4/4 marks awarded. a** The answer is well structured around two problems, both of which are focused on methodology. **b** Note that one problem applies to the person-centred approach in general and **c** the other is specific to Maslow. **d** While it is perfectly acceptable to give two general problems it does create the impression of sound knowledge to offer a combination of both a general problem and a specific one. **e** The problem of case studies gets 2 marks; the problem of using findings from individuals is identified, expanded and the student notes the implications for generalisation. **f** The second problem of subjectivity is addressed in some detail. This answer gets the full 4 marks.

(b) The cognitive approach identifies human behaviour as being similar to that of a computer. This means that humans input information and then output a response. The term 'mediational processes' refers to the processing section in between the stimulus and the response. These processes determine what the response or behaviour to a particular stimulus will be. Stimulus–response connections vary depending on mediational processes **a**. Examples of such processes are perception, attention and memory **b**. These are essential to a response and may alter responses. For example, when riding a bike on a wet road, the stimulus of the bike is the same but a key mediational process — memory — will cue you into adjusting your pedalling response (perhaps slower) to cope with the wet conditions or to remind you to adapt the way you balance so as not to fall off the bike **c**.

ⓔ **4/4 marks awarded. a** This answer demonstrates very good knowledge and understanding of mediational processes, conveying the idea that these come between stimulus and response and how they mediate between these, e.g. determining and altering the response. **b** Examples of named processes are provided but as the student has already earned the maximum AO1 marks, these do not gain credit. **c** The answer also gains 2 AO2 marks for the use of an example to illustrate the role of memory in mediating between stimulus and response.

(c) The behaviourists were influenced by empiricist philosophy; the belief that all knowledge comes from the environment and direct experience **b**. Watson started the behaviourist movement in 1913. He and others developed theories of learning,

e.g. classical and operant conditioning, which they believed could explain all behaviour. Cognitive psychologists compare the human mind to a computer, suggesting that we are information processors and that psychology should focus on studying internal mental processes **c**.

Behaviourists believe that if psychology is to be a true science, it should only concern itself with observable behaviour. Theories of learning (classical and operant conditioning) investigate learning by measuring observable responses to stimuli **f**. In classical conditioning, for example, reflex responses, such as the amount of saliva produced in response to a bell, is measured both before and after being associated with food **d**. Behavioural S–R theory therefore lends itself to the experimental approach, though often experiments are done on animals for practical reasons **h**. The cognitive approach, like the behaviourist approach, also aspires to be scientific, so measures overt behaviour such as the number of words remembered in a test of memory but from this inferring the unobservable cognitive processes. So cognitive psychology also claims to be scientific; cognitive researchers carry out controlled experiments on internal processes such as memory, perception and attention **f**.

Whereas behaviourism concentrates totally on observable overt behaviour, the cognitive approach has addressed the yawning gap between stimuli and responses created by the behaviourists and has focused on the internal processes that come in between. These internal mediating processes are covert, unlike the overt behaviour studied by the behaviourist approach. It disagrees with the behaviourists, who argue that such topics are best ignored just because they are not overt **i**.

Research into insight learning illustrates just how important it is not to ignore these processes. A hungry chimp tried to reach a banana outside its cage. After stretching unsuccessfully, it suddenly reached for a stick (also outside the cage) and used it to rake in the banana **e**. In the behaviourists' view, learning happens through association between stimulus and response, when the animal produces the correct response and is reinforced for doing so. However, in insight learning, a sudden solution appears without prior reinforcement. Cognitive psychologists point out that the activity is entirely cognitive, involving memory and perceptual restructuring, whereas behaviourists struggle, trying to explain what happens, as they believe that learning can be explained without resorting to cognitive activity **g**.

The work into insight learning points out another difference between the behaviourists and cognitive psychologists. Behaviourists are reductionist, believing that all behaviour can be explained and reduced to S–R links, whereas the cognitive approach is holistic. Insight learning is best explained by the Gestalt principles of 'the whole is greater than the sum of its parts'. This means the solution to a problem comes when all the bits are seen in relation to one another as a meaningful 'whole', which is how cognitive psychologists explain insight learning **j**.

Both approaches have their practical uses, though as their assumptions are so different, the way they apply solutions differs. For example, when looking at causes of atypical behaviour, cognitive psychologists will base their explanations on unrealistic or irrational thoughts and beliefs, whereas behaviourists would explain atypical behaviour by the learning of maladaptive responses **k**. These theoretical assumptions influence treatments. For the behaviourists, preferred treatments are behaviour therapy or behaviour modification to change behaviour, whereas cognitive psychologists aim to restructure the maladaptive thought processes l. However, the two approaches have merged to produce cognitive behaviour therapy; this combines behaviour therapy methods with techniques designed to change the way a person thinks about themselves and events. So, though the two approaches differ in terms of basic assumptions, in fact there is complementarity and overlap between them. Perhaps, for the future development of psychology, it is more productive to look at complementarity and overlap rather than the differences between them **m a**.

e **11/12 marks awarded (AO1 = 4, AO2 = 7). a** This is an organised, balanced and well-focused answer. It demonstrates breadth and depth of response, is mostly relevant and has well-structured arguments throughout. The student demonstrates a synoptic grasp of the subject, incorporating debates and topics. Substantiating arguments this way is a crucial characteristic of a good answer. **b** The following points were given credit for description: the philosophical roots of behaviourism; **c** the cognitive computer analogy; **d** the descriptions of classical conditioning **e** and insight learning. There is perhaps slight imbalance, with more emphasis on the behaviourist approach than the cognitive approach. **f** The application of the scientific method by both approaches was awarded AO2 credit plus **g** further AO2 credit for use of evidence in relation to conditioning and memory. **h** The reference to the use of animals is not relevant so no credit was given here, **i** but comparison between the behaviourist S–R approach and the cognitive approach with its mediating variables is creditworthy. **j** The introduction of insight learning presented an opportunity for further AO2 credit: for the link to the reductionism-holism debate. Finally, comparison in respect of the **k** causes of atypical behaviour, **l** treatments of this behaviour and the **m** overlap between treatments/approaches all gained AO2 credit.

Taken as a whole, this was a well thought out and analytical answer. Although more differences than similarities were discussed, the student drew the discussion to a logical close, considering the overlap and complementarity between the approaches. The only irrelevant point was the fleeting reference to animal studies. However, this is inconsequential to the answer and does not affect the credit awarded.

Total for this question: 19 out of 20 marks — grade A.

Question 3 Debates in psychology (1)

(a) Explain why some psychologists believe that the study of overt behaviour is the only way to gain knowledge about people.

(4 marks)

ⓔ It is quite possible that at least one question in the debates section will assess your knowledge and understanding of 'how science works'. In this question you are required to demonstrate your understanding of overt behaviour as being objective and how this relates to science. Notice that there are 4 marks for this question, so you need to write about and elaborate four brief points, including what 'overt behaviour' means and how the study of such behaviour applies to scientific enquiry.

(b) With reference to one example of behaviour, explain what is meant by environmental determinism.

(4 marks)

ⓔ In this part, you are required to do two things. First of all, explain what is meant by environmental determinism. Be careful to concentrate on the 'environmental' aspect and make sure that you do not talk about biological determinism. Second, refer to one example of behaviour. It is surprising how often students fail to respond to a second requirement in a question and automatically lose half the marks. You could refer to an approach, most likely the behaviourist approach, though make sure you include behaviour. Good examples of behaviour to use here would be social psychology examples, such as obedience and conformity. The example needs to convey environmental determinism and this must be fully explained.

(c) Discuss the nature–nurture debate in psychology. Refer to at least one topic area in your answer.

(12 marks)

ⓔ This section requires an extended answer and you will be assessed on the quality of your written communication as well as the psychological content. In this question, the bulk of the marks are for discussion, so focus on analysis, application and evaluation. One third of the marks are reserved for knowledge and understanding, which can include an outline of the nature–nurture debate. It is a good idea to use specialist terminology, such as concordance rates, as this will also gain marks if used appropriately. Remember to refer to at least one topic. This gives you the opportunity to show application and analysis and generally to demonstrate how this philosophical debate relates to psychology. Finally, be aware that if you do not refer to a topic then you cannot get more than 8 marks.

Student A

(a) Some psychologists, specifically scientifically minded ones **a**, are likely to record observable behaviour **b** as the only appropriate information for their investigations, as this is the only behaviour which can be acknowledged and recorded **c**. Conscious and unconscious mental processes cannot possibly provide any raw data which could be analysed **d**. Mental processes can only be known if participants explain them, so are not scientific or empirical and therefore play no part in the scientific approach **e**. Any results which are not scientific are not psychology.

🙂 **2/4 marks awarded. a** The student immediately identifies the scientific link, which is the correct context for the answer. **b** The student also refers to 'observable' behaviour, thus showing an understanding of 'overt', meaning observable. One mark is given for the observable and scientific link. **c** It is a pity that the expansion in the reference to 'acknowledged and recorded' is unclear.

If the student had been more specific, using appropriate terminology, such as referring to objectivity or verification by others, then a second mark could have been awarded. **d** The reference to conscious and unconscious mental processes suggests that the student is trying to contrast overt behaviour with private experience, though again this is not really clear. **e** The only creditworthy point, in what remains of the answer, is the reference to science and empiricism.

(b) Determinism means that an event is determined **a** and the person is not in control or responsible for their behaviour **b**. Environmental determinism means that behaviour is determined by something in the environment, like stopping at a red traffic light **c**.

🙂 **2/4 marks awarded. a** The explanation of determinism as 'determined' is a common failing. Rather than using the word 'determined', the student could have used 'caused'. **b** However, I mark is given for the idea that a person is not responsible and not in control of their behaviour. **c** The link to behaviour could well be on the right lines but is too brief to earn more than 1 mark. The student could have expanded on 'stopping at a red light' as conditioned behaviour determined by rewards and punishments.

(c) The nature–nurture debate is a debate concerning the relative contributions of the environment and genes towards our behaviour. The biological approach favours the nature side of the debate and the behaviourist approach favours the nurture side **e**.

　　The debate has been applied to autism **i** through the use of twin studies. It was found that the prevalence of autism was higher in brothers and sisters who were brought up in the same environment than adopted siblings brought up in the same environment **b**. This shows that there is a genetic link to autism, supporting the nature side of the debate **j**. However, just because siblings (including twins) share the same environment, it does not mean that differences in their behaviour are just due to their genes. The difference could be due to their unshared environment **k**, e.g. their friends **d**. So there could be some evidence that the environment plays a role in the prevalence of autism **h**.

　　The nature–nurture debate has also been used to find the contribution of the environment and genes towards schizophrenia **i**. A 48% prevalence rate **c** for schizophrenia was found between identical twins, which was higher than 17% for non-identical twins **f** and suggests that there is a genetic link to schizophrenia **l**. However, if it was just genetic then we would expect the prevalence rate to be 100%. This is not the case, so there must be something else that causes schizophrenia **m**. Some psychologists have suggested that the best way to explain the high but not perfect prevalence in identical twins is through an interaction of nature and nurture. This means that there might be a biological tendency but this has to interact with, or be brought out by, the environment **g**. So a person might inherit genes for schizophrenia, making them vulnerable, but this might only be realised if the person also suffers some stress **n**. This would explain the high but not perfect prevalence in twins as different people. Even two identical twins living in the same home may have different unshared experiences. This shows that it is very important to think of nature and nurture interacting with one another. When this happens it is not possible to say that schizophrenia is caused by genes, nor is it possible to say that it is caused by the environment **o**.

In conclusion, the nature–nurture debate is complex — this is shown by autism and schizophrenia. Both nature and nurture are involved, so an interactionist approach should be considered. **a**

(e) **8/12 marks awarded (AO1 = 3, AO2 = 5). a** This answer shows sound knowledge and understanding. Ideas are presented clearly and the response is mostly well organised. **b** The only exception is the second paragraph, which opens with twin studies but then goes on to discuss family studies and siblings in general. **c** Better use could have been made of terminology such as 'concordance rates' rather than 'prevalence rates' and of topic areas. **d** The example of friends as an environmental factor in autism is unconvincing.

AO1 credit was awarded for the following: **e** the outline of the debate in the opening paragraph; **f** the description of evidence for schizophrenia (reference to 48% and 17% 'prevalence rates'); **g** knowledge of 'interaction' between nature and nurture. **h** Note that no AO1 marks were awarded for the insubstantial evidence in relation to autism which is too vague — there is no identifiable study and no definite findings.

i Efforts at analysis and evaluation were reasonably successful and the references to autism and schizophrenia satisfied the requirement to refer to at least one topic area. **j** Some good use was made of evidence for autism, 'this shows that there is a genetic link to autism supporting the nature side of the debate'. AO2 credit was awarded for this and **k** also for the observation that shared environments cannot be assumed to mean the same environment. **l** No credit was awarded for the use of evidence in relation to schizophrenia as the analysis did not extend to the debate, only to genes. **m** However, the point about the 'prevalence rate' not being 100% and therefore another factor must be involved, was creditworthy. **n** Further credit was awarded for applying the interaction between nature and nurture to schizophrenia, and **o** for the implications of this interaction: 'When this happens it is not possible to say that schizophrenia is caused by genes, nor is it possible to say that it is caused by the environment.'

This is a solid second band response. It is logical and focused, demonstrating knowledge and understanding, analysis and application in more or less equal measure.

Total for this question: 12 out of 20 marks — grade C.

Student B

(a) The psychologists who wish to study only observable behaviour want to gain empirical evidence to show if their hypotheses are correct **a**. With empirical evidence, definite and objective answers are given about what is being studied **b** and so the results are not open to interpretation and debate. Behaviour that is not overt, such as subjective experience **c**, is subject to bias **d** and other factors that are certain to have some form of effect on the results gained. Studies using subjective experience can also be interpreted in such a way as to lend weight to theories, and these studies are not truly open to replication **e**, a major factor in the scientific approach.

ⓔ **4/4 marks awarded. a** The student has correctly recognised that overt means observable and uses psychological terminology, 'empirical', to convey the link to science. One mark is awarded for appropriate use of the term. **b** The expansion serves to explain why the study of overt behaviour is so important: '…objective answers are given about what is being studied…', thus gaining another mark. **c** Because the question asks why some psychologists consider the study of overt behaviour to be the *only* way to gain knowledge about people, the contrast with subjective experience is pertinent. The point is not very clear but conveys enough information to merit 2 marks **d** for identifying bias as a problem for scientific enquiry and **e** the implication for replication.

(b) Determinism means that behaviour is caused by factors beyond a person's control **b**. The person is therefore not responsible for the behaviour. Environmental determinism relates to factors in the environment being responsible for behaviour, as put forward by the behaviourists. They claimed that behaviour is under the control of reinforcement and punishment **c**. An example is gambling. To most people, gambling is a choice made by a person. They have the free will **d** to gamble or not to gamble and are responsible for the behaviour. However, according to behaviourists and environmental determinism, the person does not have free will. The reason for the behaviour is due to its consequences, for example, the occasional win. The person is totally at the mercy of the environment **e a**.

ⓔ **4/4 marks awarded a** This is a detailed and accurate answer which deals effectively with both requirements of the question. **b** Environmental determinism is explained using appropriate terminology; marks are awarded for correctly stating that behaviour is caused by factors beyond a person's control and **c** for the elaboration of reinforcement and punishment. **d** The example of gambling is appropriate and works well, illustrating the debate and the view that gambling could quite easily be attributed to free will. **e** The application of behaviourist principles through discussion of the consequences (the occasional win) is convincing, so 2 marks are given for the example.

(c) The nature–nurture debate is a philosophical debate that pre-dates psychology. Nature refers to the fact that our behaviour is because of our genes, instincts and the attributes that we are born with. Nurture refers to behaviour as the result of our upbringing, learning and experience; the environment we have grown up in. The debate concerns the relative contributions of nature and nurture in behaviour. Is behaviour mainly due to the environment or mainly due to our nature? **d**

Psychodynamic theory suggests that all actions are the result of unconscious processes and the most powerful of these, which drive behaviour, are instincts. The theory therefore emphasises the role of nature in development. However, Freud also argues that parents have a huge impact on personality, thus pointing to the role of nurture as well **e**. A similar mix of nature and nurture in behaviour is the theory of Piaget. Like Freud, he emphasises the nature aspect, except that Piaget does not consider unconscious instincts but rather biological maturation, universal invariant processes of assimilation and accommodation, and an inborn tendency to adapt to the environment. However, because the child has to interact with an environment in order to develop schema, then the environment (nurture) also plays a role in development **b f**.

It is not possible to investigate the nature–nurture debate in any empirical way as it applies to Piaget and to Freud. Freud's theory of the unconscious instincts does not lend itself to experiments and it would be unethical to test Piaget's theory by separating a baby from its environment **i**. However, the Koluchova study suggests that nurture is very important. Czech twins, who had been deprived of all stimulation and were significantly cognitively retarded, once schooled for a year, developed fast and caught up with their peers **g**. This shows that nurture plays a role in cognitive development **h**.

The topic of substance abuse shows the debate in action. Here there is some attempt to assess the relative contributions of nature and nurture. Some psychologists argue that people who abuse substances have a genetic predisposition to do so. It has been shown that offspring of alcoholics are ten times more likely to become an alcoholic, suggesting that nature does play a role **k**. The problem, though, with this argument is that it is possible that nurture could also explain the finding and that the environment in which the child grew up, including the presence of an alcoholic role model, moulded the child into an alcoholic **l**. Adoption studies, however, have shown that adopted children of alcoholics (adopted into the home of non-alcoholics) are more likely to become abusers themselves than adopted children whose biological parents do not abuse. This strongly implicates nature in alcohol abuse **c j m**.

More recently, psychologists are leaning towards an interactionist approach, pointing out that both nature and nurture interact in behaviour. It is impossible and too simplistic to separate the two **n**. For example, you may be genetically predisposed to abuse alcohol, but it needs to be available for you to become an alcoholic **o**. Also, social norms can lead to abuse of substances. This does not mean that everyone will abuse, although if you are genetically predisposed then this makes you more vulnerable. Perhaps nature makes it more likely that 'bad' nurture will take effect and 'good' nature makes it less likely **p**.

The debate is not simply a philosophical debate but is very relevant to scientific psychology. The questions it raises are very important, as an understanding of the role of nature and nurture has implications for the control of behaviour such as informing social policy **a q**.

(e) 11/12 marks awarded **(AO1 = 4, AO2 = 7). a** The answer is well constructed and well focused. It demonstrates both breadth and depth of response, is relevant and with well-structured arguments throughout. The student demonstrates a synoptic grasp of the subject, applying the debate to a number of topics. **b** The answer becomes a little formulaic when applied to Piaget, though good use is made of both Piagetian and Freudian theory. **c** The topic of substance abuse is used effectively to demonstrate analysis and application.

d Credit was given for knowledge and understanding of nature, nurture and of the debate. **e** Further AO1 credit was awarded for relevant aspects of nature and nurture in both Freud's and **f** Piaget's theories. **g** Credit could have been gained for the description of evidence (the deprivation study), had the maximum not already been achieved. **h** However, credit was given for the use of this evidence. **i** This was preceded by credit for analysis of the difficulties of scientifically investigating the debate, as applied to both Piaget and Freud. **j** The topic of substance abuse generated credit as follows: **k** use of evidence ('It has been shown that offspring of alcoholics are ten times more likely to become an alcoholic, suggesting that nature does play a role'); **l** arguing that findings could just as easily be explained by environmental factors or nurture; **m** presentation of evidence to draw the argument to a conclusion.

n The point that it is too simplistic and not possible to separate nature and nurture is not explained and **o** even the example does not help. **p** However, what the example does do is to illustrate the interaction between nature and nurture in substance abuse, which is creditworthy.

q Concluding paragraphs are rarely creditworthy, as usually information is simply repeated or a throw-away, unsubstantiated comment such as the need for a more eclectic approach is made. However, in this answer the student has cleverly made a very relevant point about the implications of the debate. Considering such broader issues and appreciating the ways in which society uses science to inform decision-making is the mark of a good answer, and earns further credit.

Total for this question: 19 out of 20 marks — grade A.

Question 4 Debates in psychology (II)

(a) Explain why reductionism is compatible with the idea of psychology as a science. (4 marks)

(e) The answer must be set in the context of science. You will need to get across the meaning of the term 'reductionism' and explain why reductionism relates to science. If it helps, use an example of a reductionist explanation of behaviour. As there are 4 marks available for this question, make sure you expand your answer. You can, of course, contrast reductionism with holism if relevant to the explanation.

(b) Briefly discuss one strength of the idiographic approach in psychology. (4 marks)

(e) This is a straightforward question but requires more than a simple description. A discussion requires some kind of evaluation, application or analysis. The first thing to do is to identify one strength. State this clearly and make sure that you select one that you can discuss. All too often, students write down the first thing that comes into their heads but then find that there is not much to discuss. One way of tackling this is to evaluate by comparing the idiographic with the nomothetic approach. Another is to demonstrate analysis and application by using an example. Do not make the mistake of identifying more than one strength to compensate for a lack of discussion. This is not a good strategy as it wastes time and you will only be credited for one.

(c) Discuss at least two limitations of the scientific approach in psychology. Refer to examples from psychology in your answer. (12 marks)

(e) This question requires an extended answer and you will be assessed on the quality of your written communication as well as the psychological content. In this question, the bulk of the marks are for discussion, so focus on analysis, application and evaluation. 4 marks are for knowledge and understanding of the (two) limitations. Remember to cover at least two; you will gain a maximum of 7 marks if you only cover one. Refer to examples, as this gives you the opportunity to show application and analysis. Do not write about scientific methodology alone as this is just one aspect of the scientific approach. Try to include philosophical issues, such as determinism, reductionism and the nomothetic approach, where relevant to the discussion. You can bring in ethical issues and refer to approaches such as the humanistic approach and the rejection of science. Beware of misconceptions in questions on the scientific approach. The scientific approach is not confined to the laboratory experiment and non-experimental methods can also lack ecological validity.

Student A

(a) Reductionism is reducing a complex set of phenomena into a basic simple form. This is a necessary part of enabling us to understand processes **b** and is more scientific than holism, which is looking at individuals as a whole **a**.

(e) **2/4 marks awarded. a** The student clearly has some knowledge and understanding of reductionism and holism. This information merits 1 mark. **b** The link between science and the necessity for reductionism is just about enough to merit a second mark. This answer lacks convincing explanation and so gains no more than 2 marks.

(b) The idiographic approach to psychology looks at the unique experiences of the individual and is more subjective and qualitative than the nomothetic approach **b d**. Its main strength is that it looks at the whole person **c**. It takes into account subjective feelings and does not attempt to generalise across all people **e**. As such, richer and more ecologically valid data is likely to be obtained with the idiographic approach **f a**.

ⓔ **2/4 marks awarded. a** There are several valid points here but these are not applied effectively in answer to the question. **b** The first sentence does not get any credit because it is not clear whether or not the points made are referring to a strength of the approach. **c** The second sentence does make a clear statement about the strength of the approach and so gains credit. **d** The points about the idiographic approach being subjective, qualitative and **e** not capable of generalisation, are features of the approach and are not used to elaborate on the strength (the whole person), so do not gain credit. **f** The final sentence, which is an evaluative point, is creditworthy.

(c) The scientific approach is good in that it considers control, cause and effect. This means that it investigates how the independent variable affects the dependent variable and helps us in understanding why things happen **b**.

Yet, although it does this, it dehumanises the participants. People are seen as objects of study. An example of this is seen in the social psychology studies of obedience to authority. Participants were put into situations where they had to deliver electric shocks to another human being. The experimenter ordered them to deliver shocks, even though they were very distressed, and observed how they behaved **g j q**.

Another problem with the scientific method in psychology is experimenter bias. This is where the experimenter knows the outcome wanted and in some way makes this happen. This may be by things such as the way in which he acts with the participants **e k**. The problem is that this makes the data unreliable and you cannot generalise from it.

Another problem is demand characteristics. Unlike chemicals, people are individuals, capable of cognition. When they are involved in psychological studies, they often try to guess what the study is about and behave accordingly. This is because participants are in strange surroundings and they feel they should act in a certain way **f l**. This is seen in the Asch study on conformity, where participants were in a strange situation with a group of actors, and asked to say which line was the longest. The participants began to conform to the group who gave the wrong answer because they were unsure what else to do. When asked later, many participants said that they thought that was the way they were expected to behave because the rest of the group had **h o r**.

There are problems with studies like Asch's, as ethical guidelines say participants should be protected **t**. Nowadays, all research conforms to the BPS guide and so some experiments cannot be done. This is a major problem for psychology **d m**.

The scientific approach involves laboratory procedures; these are low in ecological validity and therefore participants may not act like they would in the real world **p s**. It looks at humans as if they are machines, which is a problem as humans are beings with free will **n**. The humanistic approach rejects science for this very reason **c u**.

Psychology doesn't share a common paradigm which is characteristic of other natural sciences. Grey argues that this is because it is a young science and psychologists now support the cognitive perspective **i a**.

ⓔ **7/12 marks awarded (AO1 = 3, AO2 = 4).** **a** This answer shows reasonable knowledge and understanding of the scientific approach, though **b** regrettably the answer strongly implies that the scientific approach is limited to laboratory procedures. This is conveyed by the first and **c** penultimate (second to last) paragraphs. **d** Generally, limitations are presented clearly and, on the whole, the answer is well organised. **e** There is some evidence of appropriate psychological terminology, e.g. experimenter bias and **f** demand characteristics. **g h** The student makes some good use of studies but analysis and application is lacking for a top band answer. **i** The last paragraph is totally redundant and is veering towards the question 'is psychology a science?' Credit for knowledge and understanding can be awarded for each of the following limitations: **j** the dehumanising aspect of the scientific approach (it is always safer to explicitly state that this is a limitation but fortunately there is enough context and elaboration to convey that this is a limitation); **k** experimenter bias, which was explicitly stated and outlined; **l** demand characteristics; **m** ethical issues; **n** people as machines. Only 4 AO1 marks could be awarded for these five points. **o** Notice that no credit was given for the description of the Asch study, as it was neither quite detailed enough nor accurate. **p** The point about ecological validity did not gain credit either, as it was not stated as a limitation/problem but as a fact. **q** There is some good use made of evidence in the answer. Credit was awarded for application of dehumanisation to Milgram, which was quite well done and conveyed the idea of participants as 'objects of study'. **r** Credit was awarded to the Asch study for linking demand characteristics to the behaviour of the participants and for use of evidence ('when asked later…'). **s** There are, however, some missed opportunities for marks. Ecological validity and **t** ethical issues could also have been applied to examples, **u** and the final limitation, people as machines, could have generated quite a discussion, especially as the student had linked it to free will and the humanistic approach.

This is a reasonably solid second band response. It is logical and focused, demonstrating knowledge and understanding but lacks the analysis and application for a really convincing answer.

Total for this question: 11 out of 20 marks — grade D.

Student B

(a) Reductionist explanations are simple, parsimonious explanations which reduce complex phenomena down to basic components **b**. These can be used to guide theory and research **c**. An example is understanding learning by looking at stimulus–response connections. Because reductionist explanations explain even complex learning by the simplest underlying principles possible, S–R associations, it is possible to test these **d**. Using reductionist explanations, psychology gains scientific credibility **e**. Holistic explanations **f**, on the other hand, consider the 'whole' picture which makes it difficult to determine what is causing the behaviour and to apply scientific methods of research **a**.

ⓔ **4/4 marks awarded. a** This is a clear, concise answer which deals with the requirements of the question. **b** Reductionism is explained using appropriate terminology (parsimonious means economical). The first sentence therefore merits 1 mark. **c** The point that these basic components or principles guide theory and research is a creditworthy point, linking reductionism to science. **d** Another mark is given to the S–R example, which is used effectively to illustrate the point. **e** The reference to scientific credibility, though valid, is not relevant, so does not gain credit. **f** The contrast with holistic explanations adds to the explanation, bringing the total to 4 marks.

(b) A strength of the idiographic approach is that it takes into account the whole person, an individual's feelings and experiences **a**, which in some cases is better than the nomothetic approach for gaining a fuller picture of the individual **b**. However, this cannot be generalised to others **c**. For example, in the case of aggression, an idiographic approach would involve an in-depth look at what causes aggression for a particular person. This could lead to help for that person, rather than assuming that everyone who has an aggressive nature has the same problem or that it is caused by the same factors **d e**.

ⓔ **4/4 marks awarded. a** This student launches straight into a strength, which is a good strategy, particularly with short questions where time is of the essence. One mark for the strength is **b** followed by a second mark for elaboration and comparison with the nomothetic approach. **c** The point about lack of generalisability is a valid analytical point. Fortunately, the student does not change the focus of the answer to limitations and quickly returns to the strength of the approach, **d** cleverly using an example of behaviour and linking this to practical applications of the approach. **e** This is a thoughtful, well-constructed answer that gains full marks.

(c) In considering the assumptions of science, the first problem is that of determinism. The scientific approach looks for cause and effect in every aspect of human behaviour and therefore assumes that people are predictable and controllable **j**. Also, the scientific approach takes a reductionist view, assuming that complex behaviour can be reduced down to basic components **k**. Such a narrow focus when investigating causes of behaviour does not do justice to the complexity of human behaviour. Humanistic psychologists argue for a more holistic approach. The problems of scientific reductionism and determinism can be seen in the biological approach to understanding gender and criminal behaviour. One biological theory is that gender-related aggression and criminality can be explained by levels of hormones. Dabbs et al. (1995) studied the link between prisoners' behaviour, their crime and their testosterone levels. Testing prisoners' saliva and looking at prison records, a link was found between level of testosterone and type of crime. The researchers established that the higher the level of testosterone, the more aggressive the crime, thus linking testosterone with aggression and crime **c l q**. However, such a reductionist explanation ignores the effects of social and environmental factors, as well as the interaction between the biological, psychological and environmental factors. **r** The study also illustrates the other problem with the scientific approach, that of determinism. Because the scientific approach looks for causes of behaviour, it cannot accommodate free will. Even if high levels of testosterone predispose a person to aggressiveness, people do have free will and are morally responsible; the human

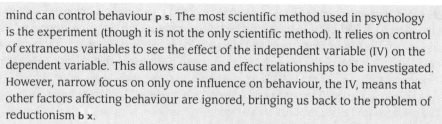

mind can control behaviour **p s**. The most scientific method used in psychology is the experiment (though it is not the only scientific method). It relies on control of extraneous variables to see the effect of the independent variable (IV) on the dependent variable. This allows cause and effect relationships to be investigated. However, narrow focus on only one influence on behaviour, the IV, means that other factors affecting behaviour are ignored, bringing us back to the problem of reductionism **b x**.

There are also problems with the method itself. Tight controls alter the behaviour being measured, leading to low ecological validity and unnatural behaviour **m**. Examples of research with low ecological validity are typical memory studies, e.g. on the role of interference in forgetting. Such experiments often involve learning lists of word pairs or nonsense words, so hardly reflecting normal everyday forgetting **d t**.

Unlike other sciences, the object of study in psychology is the same species as the researcher. Objectivity is a problem in all sciences as researcher effects can influence outcomes. Kuhn (1970) believed that total objectivity was never possible because the view that any researcher holds about the world makes them think about it in a specific way. **n** This influences what is investigated, the methods used, and in psychology can result in the problem of experimenter expectations which affect the participants who search for clues about how to behave. This is known as demand characteristics **g**. One way round this problem is to use the double-blind technique, where neither experimenter nor participants know what is happening **f u y**.

A final general point about limitations of the scientific approach is that of testability. Much of the subject matter of psychology is unobservable and therefore cannot be accurately measured **h**. Out of all the sciences it is probably the most inferential **i**. An example is Freud's theory of psychosexual development, where many of the key ideas are neither testable nor falsifiable **e o v**.

It is incorrect to assume that the limitations of the scientific approach only relate to the experiment. The real problems with the scientific approach, as applied to psychology, are the various assumptions it holds such as determinism, reductionism and objectivity and these apply to most methods of research in varying degrees **w a**.

ⓔ 12/12 marks awarded (AO1 = 4, AO2 = 8). a The answer is well constructed and well focused. It demonstrates breadth and depth of response, is relevant, and contains well-structured arguments. **b** Limitations are not simply stated but elaborated to reveal an excellent grasp of the topic. An example of this can be seen in the opening paragraph, where the student elaborates on the problems of both determinism and reductionism. **c** The synoptic grasp of the subject is made clear by references to several examples from psychology, such as gender-related aggression and crime, **d** memory and **e** Freud. **f** Specialist terminology is used appropriately throughout, e.g. double-blind, **g** demand characteristics, **h** testability and **i** inferential.

Credit for knowledge and understanding was awarded as follows: **j** determinism; **k** reductionism; **l** the Dabbs study; **m** low ecological validity. Further credit could have been awarded for identifying problems with **n** objectivity and **o** testability. AO2 credit was given for application and analysis as follows: **p** application of reductionism and determinism to criminal behaviour; **q** use of evidence (Dabbs); **r** the problem of a reductionist explanation of criminal behaviour; **s** the issue of free will and moral responsibility; **t** memory research used to illustrate the problem of low ecological validity; **u** the discussion of objectivity, experimenter expectations and demand characteristics; **v** the inferential nature of psychology and the link to Freud; **w** the analytical observation about the assumptions of psychology applying to all methods of research in the final paragraph.

This is a very good answer. There are only two minor improvements that could have been made. First, **x** the point about the narrow focus on one variable could have been applied to an example from psychology. **y** Second, the argument about objectivity, experimenter effects and demand characteristics could have been structured more coherently. This opens with the point that humans are the objects of study, moves on to experimenter expectations and then goes back to the 'objects of study' and the problem of demand characteristics. Nevertheless, 12 out of 12 marks is appropriate overall.

Total for this question: 20 out of 20 marks — grade A.

Questions & Answers

Question 5 **Methods in psychology (1)**

A health psychologist wished to discover whether or not a strong sense of self-efficacy reduces perceived job stress. Self-efficacy is a person's belief that they can succeed at something they want to do. The hypothesis for the study was: 'the stronger the sense of self-efficacy, the lower the job stress reported'.

The study involved a sample of 30 individuals in a variety of occupations who responded to a newspaper advertisement. The psychologist arranged for one researcher to administer a job stress questionnaire. The researcher asked each participant to rate ten statements on a 7-point scale. The statements were related to stress at work during the previous 3 months. This measure gave an overall stress score. The higher the score, the greater the experience of stress.

A second researcher later administered and scored a self-efficacy questionnaire given to the same 30 individuals. The higher the score achieved, the stronger the sense of self-efficacy.

Both researchers were unaware of the hypothesis being tested. All participants were tested individually. The scores from each of the questionnaires given to the 30 individuals are shown in the scattergram.

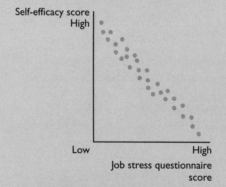

Scattergram to show the relationship between scores from the job stress questionnaire and the self-efficacy questionnaire

(a) The psychologist used volunteers for this study. Identify *one* advantage and *one* disadvantage of using volunteers in psychological research. (2 marks)

Although a brief answer is needed, the skill is to write enough to convey the advantage and disadvantage clearly. To ensure that your answer is informed and not simply common sense, you should refer to your knowledge of sampling techniques. Use psychological terminology where possible, for example, 'generalising' results.

(b) Name and describe the type of relationship which is indicated by the scattergram. (2 marks)

ⓔ There are two aspects to this question. The first is simply to state the type of relationship or correlation. There are only three types and most students can recognise these from a scattergram. The second aspect is quite straightforward too. You need to describe the trend for each variable and compare these. Take care to be precise in your answer.

(c) Name an appropriate statistical test that the psychologist could have used to see if there is a significant relationship between the job-stress score and the self-efficacy score. Justify your answer.   (3 marks)

ⓔ This is a common question so you must know and understand the criteria for the selection of tests. Students sometimes draw a table they have memorised for this type of question and you may find this helpful. Once you have selected the test, you need to give at least two reasons for the decision in order to get the full 3 marks. Think in terms of the design, the level of measurement and whether or not the research is investigating a relationship between two variables or a difference. If you have named the wrong test, you can still get credit for the reasons if these are correct.

(d) Neither of the researchers who administered the questionnaires was told about the research hypothesis. Explain why this might have been an important aspect of the study.   (2 marks)

ⓔ This question is about removing bias, so you need to say this to get full marks. However, even if you do not use this terminology, you will still get a mark if your answer is reasonably correct and conveys the sense of bias. Use of terminology such as 'double blind' will impress the examiner but is not essential to achieve full marks here.

(e) Identify *one* methodological limitation of the study. Briefly explain how the psychologist could improve the design of the study to take account of this limitation.   (3 marks)

ⓔ You need to think about this question in two parts. First identify a methodological limitation. Do not go for the first thing that comes to mind, but choose a limitation that will allow you to explain confidently how you could improve the design of the study. Be specific; do not talk in general terms about 'getting a bigger and better sample including people of different ages, from different cultures and a variety of work situations', unless you can really explain how you could practically do this, which is unlikely. The examiner should have enough detail to be able to implement your suggestion. Notice also that you are asked how to improve the design and not asked to explain the limitation. Finally, a word of caution; methodological limitations do not include ethical issues.

(f) Briefly discuss *one* strength and *one* limitation of correlational studies in psychology.   (4 marks)

ⓔ Try to deliver a balanced answer. There are 2 marks each for the strength and limitation, so make sure that you address each in more or less equal measure. If you find it difficult to develop your discussion then use an example from psychology to illustrate your answer.

(g) The psychologist has asked you to check the validity of the self-efficacy questionnaire. Outline *one* way in which you could do this. Include in your answer sufficient detail to allow for reasonable replication of the procedure. Refer to use of statistical analysis in your answer.   (4 marks)

ⓔ This question is testing your knowledge of 'how science works'. You will need to outline the entire procedure step by step. The person reading this needs to be able to replicate the procedure,

so consider what information they would need to know to be able to do so. The answer must be accurate; use appropriate terminology and refer to statistical analyses.

Student A

(a) One advantage of using volunteers is that the people who take part actually want to do so. They are keen so are more likely to carry out the investigation properly **a**. One disadvantage is that the sample is not representative of the population, so the results will be harder to generalise **b** across the whole population **c**.

ⓔ **2/2 marks awarded. a** There is some evidence that volunteer samples are more motivated, so the point made is a fair one and gains 1 mark. **b** The point about volunteer samples not being representative and therefore there will be problems with generalising is also valid, gaining a second mark. **c** Although the student has gained credit for this point, you might want to bear in mind that it is far better to refer to the 'target' population than the 'whole' population.

(b) There is a strong negative correlation on the graph **a**. The higher the job stress, the higher the self-efficacy and vice versa **b**.

ⓔ **1/2 marks awarded. a** A negative correlation was correctly identified for 1 mark. **b** However, it has not been described correctly. It should read, 'the higher the job stress, the lower the self-efficacy and vice versa'. It is much easier to describe a positive correlation than a negative correlation and care must be taken to avoid such an error.

(c) The statistical test that should be used is the chi-squared test **a**, as it was a test of association or relationship **c** and the data obtained were nominal **b**.

ⓔ **1/3 marks awarded. a** The chi-squared test is often chosen incorrectly by students and it would not be appropriate here. **b** The data are not nominal but ordinal; the ratings for the two questionnaires yield ordinal data. Of course, ordinal data can be reduced to nominal, but there is no suggestion that this is what happened here. **c** 1 mark can be given for 'a test of relationship' or 'association'.

(d) If the experimenters knew the hypothesis then they might try to 'fix' the results or even cheat **b**. The opposite could also happen — 'the screw you' effect **a**.

ⓔ **1/2 marks awarded. a** The student has confused demand characteristics with experimenter bias. **b** However, 1 mark can be given for the understanding that some form of bias is more likely to occur if the experimenters are aware of the hypotheses.

(e) A limitation is that only a small sample was used **a**. Thirty people is hardly big enough **b** to be able to generalise **c**. The psychologist could improve the design by asking for more volunteers, e.g. 100 **d**.

e **0/3 marks awarded. a** This is an example of unthinkingly plumping for something with no real substance and then finding that there is not much to write about. **b** Thirty is not really a small sample, so no credit is gained for this point. **c** The issue over generalisation is really more to do with how the sample was selected rather than the size, though for very small samples, such as in case studies, it is an issue. **d** Bumping up a figure from 30 to 100 is not conveying any real knowledge and understanding of methodological issues. No marks were given for this answer.

(f) One limitation of correlation studies is that, although they provide a link between two things, they don't identify the cause and effect of the correlation **a**. One strength of correlation studies is that they provide empirical evidence which can be easily put on a graph **b**.

e **2/4 marks awarded. a** The limitation is just about worth 2 marks. It is one of those answers that sits on the border between 1 and 2 marks. The lack of a causal connection is correct for 1 mark but the context 'they provide a link between two things' for the second mark is only a hint of a discussion. **b** The strength given gets no credit. Most studies provide empirical evidence and the point about transferring data onto a graph is not relevant. The strength should be a feature that is unique to correlation studies alone.

(g) Validity is when something is measuring what it is supposed to be measuring. There are different types of validity, including face validity and ecological validity **a**. Validity can be tested using a correlation. You can find some other test of self-efficacy and then compare the findings using a correlation **b**.

e **1/4 marks awarded a** The answer contains information not required by the question, i.e. the definition and types of validity. While such information can sometimes help students structure their answers, the information itself cannot be given credit. **b** There is some relevant information on correlations and another test of self-efficacy. However, neither of these two points is developed, nor is there a real sense of 'how' validity is measured.

Total for this question: 8 out of 20 marks — approximately grade E.

Student B

(a) Using volunteers for this study would have the advantage of being a relatively **b** quick and efficient way of collecting participants. Essentially, the participants would come to them and they would not have to go and look for and ask each individual themselves **a**. A disadvantage of using volunteers is that the researcher may not obtain a representative sample of the population. Volunteers were obtained using an advertisement in a paper, so they could also have been from a particular class or group of people who read that type of paper. This means you would not be able to generalise the findings to the wider population **c**.

e **2/2 marks awarded a** The advantage is correctly stated and, though not required, elaborated. **b** Another strength of this response is that the student recognises that finding participants using this sampling technique is not simply quick and efficient but only 'relatively' so. This is quite an insightful response and the 1 mark is given for the advantage. **c** The disadvantage is also elaborated. Although not asked to refer to this study, the student has done so and made a very valid point, relating as an example the origin of the advert to the type of people who might come across it. 1 mark is also given for the disadvantage. This part of the question scores the full 2 marks. Had this been a 4-mark question, the student would have scored the full 4 marks.

> **(b)** There is a strong negative correlation **a**. As the scores on the sense of self-efficacy increase, so the job-stress scores decrease **b**.

ⓔ **2/2 marks awarded. a** The type of correlation is correctly identified and **b** described. There is no need to comment on the strength of the correlation; 'negative' alone would suffice.

> **(c)** The statistical test is the Spearman's rho **a**. This is because the data could not be treated as interval, as ratings of stress are ranked scores only so are at the ordinal level of measurement. The self-efficacy scores are estimates only, so are also ordinal **b**. The test is looking for a relationship, so Spearman's rho is appropriate: a non-parametric test of the relationship between two variables **c**.

ⓔ **3/3 marks awarded. a** The correct test was selected, for 1 mark. **b** There is detailed justification for the data being ordinal, making for a clear and informed answer most definitely deserving a mark. **c** The student also identifies that the psychologist was investigating a relationship, for the third mark.

> **(d)** This is to remove bias **a**. Experimenters may unintentionally, or even intentionally, transmit cues about their expectations and results of the experiment **b**, so it makes sense to keep them in the dark. This is known as double blind procedure as opposed to single blind, when only participants do not know what is going on.

ⓔ **2/2 marks awarded. a** 1 mark can be awarded for recognising that this is to control bias and a **b** second mark for explaining how this bias can arise. The reference to 'double blind' is both correct and looks impressive, though it is not essential.

> **(e)** All participants filled in the job-stress questionnaire first and then the self-efficacy questionnaire second. The problem here is that this same order for all participants creates a bias **a**. The psychologist could have improved the design of the study by asking alternate participants to complete the questionnaire in a different order, so half do the self-efficacy questionnaire first and the other half do the job-stress questionnaire first (a bit like counter-balancing in a repeated design experiment) **b**. Finally, the scores from each questionnaire would be compared against each other and plotted on a scattergram to examine the relationship between them **c**.

ⓔ **3/3 marks awarded. a** The student identifies and describes a possible source of bias in the method. 1 mark can therefore be given for identifying a methodological limitation. **b** There is then a clear outline of what can be done to improve the design of the study: alternate participants completing the questionnaires in reverse order; **c** analysis of results. The answer is accurate, relevant and replicable and deserves the full 2 marks for the improvement.

(f) A strength of correlation studies is that they allow variables to be investigated that would be unethical or impractical to manipulate in an experiment **a**. This though brings about a limitation of correlational studies; they can't establish cause and effect, only a link between variables **c**. However, in providing a link between variables, they can generate predictive information such as risk factors in stress **b d e**.

😊 **3/4 marks awarded. d** This answer is somewhat unbalanced, with a good attempt at dealing with the strength but little said about the limitation. **a** The point about the use of correlation studies in situations where experimental manipulation is not possible is correct and awarded 1 mark. **b** A further mark can be awarded for the analysis of this strength, which follows towards the end. **c** The limitation could have been developed by explaining that cause and effect cannot be established due to all the uncontrolled variables, or by reference to an example. **e** As it stands, only 1 mark can be given to the limitation.

(g) I will test concurrent validity **a**. The first thing is to find an 'old' established test of self-efficacy that has already been validated **b**. It is then necessary to test the same people **c**. There will now be two sets of scores: one set for the 'new' test and one set for the 'old' test **d**. The next step is to see if there is a high positive correlation between the two tests, because if the test is valid, then you should find similar scores. People who score high on self-efficacy in one test will score high on self-efficacy on the other and similarly, if they score low on one, they will score low on the other **e**. The scores can be plotted on a scattergram. Finally, I will analyse the data using a correlational test **f**. As the data are ordinal and the design related, then the test to use is Spearman's rho **g**. This will give me the correlation coefficient for the association between the two tests. This can be checked for significance using the appropriate critical values table **h**. I will record the names of the test in my report, so that the person reading it will be able to replicate the procedure **i**.

😊 **4/4 marks awarded. a** As there are different ways of testing validity, it is a good idea to do as this student has done and immediately identify the type of validity to be tested. Several relevant points follow and in the correct order: **b** an old validated test; **c** testing the same people; **d** two sets of scores; **e** positive correlation; **f** graphical and statistical analyses. **g** The statistical analysis is justified and is correct. **h** This student clearly does know how to interpret statistical outcomes by making reference to critical values tables. **i** His/her knowledge of report writing has put the finishing touches to what is already an excellent answer — the need to record the names of the tests in the report and the purpose of doing so.

Total for this question: 19 out of 20 marks — grade A.

Question 6 **Methods in psychology (II)**

The head teacher of a primary school was interested in discovering which of two methods of teaching mathematics was most preferred by pupils in the school. The head teacher also wanted to see if boys and girls differed in their preferences.

Forty boys and 40 girls aged 8–10 years were involved in the study. All the children had experienced both of the teaching methods. She asked each child which method of teaching he or she preferred, and obtained the following data:

Table 1 Numbers o f boys and girls preferring teaching method A and teaching method B

	Teaching method A	Teaching method B
Boys' preference	12	28
Girls' preference	24	16

(a) Interpret the data in Table 1. (2 marks)

 This is quite a common opening question. Always look at the mark allocation, because this will give you some indication as to how much to write and how many points to make. This question is worth 2 marks so think of two points. You should always look back to the stem of the question to remind yourself of the purpose of the study. In this piece of research, the head teacher was interested in discovering which of two methods of teaching mathematics was most liked by the pupils and if boys and girls differed in their preferences. Table 1 provides information on both of these aims.

(b) The chi-squared test was used to analyse the data. The calculated value of chi-squared (X^2) was 7.27. Using *Table 2* below, explain whether or not the result is significant. (2 marks)

(X^2) must be *equal to or more than* the stated value to be significant.

Table 2

Level of significance for a two-tailed test				
df	*0.1*	*0.05*	*0.01*	*0.001*
1	2.706	3.841	6.635	10.83

After the survey, all children were taught using teaching method A for 2 months and then tested in mathematics at the end of this period. The maximum score on the test was 100. For the next 2 months, all the children were taught using teaching method B. At the end of this period, they were tested again using a different mathematics test. This test was also out of 100. The average results for all the children on the two tests are given in Table 3 below.

Table 3 Means and standard deviations for mathematics test scores after using teaching method A and teaching method B

	After teaching method A	After teaching method B
Mean test score	57	66
Standard deviation	7.4	4.6

ⓔ This is a question that many students think they simply cannot do and therefore don't do very well on. Be prepared to interpret a statistical table. All the information is given for you. The calculated value (also known as 'obtained' or 'observed' value) is the one that you are given — literally, the one that has been calculated from the raw data. The stated or 'critical' value(s) are the table values. All you need do is compare the calculated value with the stated value and interpret the comparison in relation to levels of significance as instructed by the table. You will not get a mark simply for saying the result is or is not significant. You will need to give the level of probability.

(c) Explain why standard deviations are often used in addition to means in order to summarise data. (1 marks)

ⓔ A possible pitfall here is not reading the question properly and describing the standard deviation or comparing it with the mean. To answer this question, you need to think in terms of what the standard deviation is and what additional information it provides.

(d) The head teacher chose to use the parametric independent t-test to see if there was a significant difference between the test scores following the use of teaching method A and teaching method B. The difference in mean test scores was statistically significant at the 5% level.

(i) State _one_ advantage of using a parametric test rather than a non-parametric test. (1 marks)

ⓔ There are several advantages of parametric tests but only one needs to be stated. You need to be very clear and precise. Avoid answers such as, 'they are more accurate' which, unless qualified, is too imprecise to get a mark.

(ii) Identify _two_ criteria which must be satisfied before carrying out a parametric test. (2 marks)

ⓔ The specification requires you to know the criteria for parametric testing, which is what this question is asking for. It is a straightforward recall of knowledge. Do be careful, though, not to confuse these criteria with the process you go through when selecting a test. The type of design, for instance, is irrelevant.

(e) The head teacher believed that she had sufficient evidence to conclude that teaching method B was more effective than teaching method A.

Identify _one_ variable, other than the teaching method itself, which could account for the superior test scores following the use of teaching method B. Explain your answer. (2 marks)

ⓔ This question is about the design of the study. Specifically, it is asking you to consider if there are any obvious confounding variables which may be the cause of the differences between the test scores. You might need to read back over the design and think in terms of any variables that were allowed to vary along with the independent variable. Do not confuse confounding variables with extraneous variables and remember to explain your answer.

(f) Briefly explain *one* ethical issue raised by this study. (2 marks)

ⓔ Several ethical issues usually apply to any one study. The skill here is to select one issue only which applies to the study (do not do any more as you will only be credited for one) and which you feel that you can explain. Quite often students identify an issue which is relevant but then find they do not know how to develop their answers in relation to the study.

(g) The head teacher read about a new test which could identify potentially good teachers of mathematics. Describe *one* way of measuring the reliability of the test. (3 marks)

ⓔ Some aspect of reliability and/or validity can come up in a research methods question so make sure you are prepared for this. Use the marks here to guide you as to how much to write. For 3 marks you need to make three points. Notice also that you are not asked to define the term but to explain how reliability can be measured. Do not forget to take the measuring process right through to the end and remember to include statistical analysis.

(h) You are interested in the behaviour of primary school children during mathematics lessons and have asked to be allowed to carry out an observational study at a primary school. You have decided to work with one other psychology student.

Plan an observation of disruptive behaviour by children during their mathematics lessons. Include in your answer sufficient detail for someone to be able to implement your plan.

In your answer, refer to:
- **a category system**
- **the sampling of behaviour**
- **a check on reliability**

ethical considerations (5 marks)

ⓔ This question is testing your knowledge of 'how science works'. Always leave yourself plenty of time for this question and make sure that you do all that is asked of you. Go through each point systematically and make sure that the person reading your answer would be able to replicate the procedure. This question is asking you for a plan, so the answer may be written in plan form. Four aspects of the study are specified in the question and 5 marks are available, so you can assume that some elaboration of at least one aspect is required for the full 5 marks.

(a) Twelve of the boys preferred A and 28 preferred B. Twenty-four of the girls preferred A and 16 preferred B. Thirty-six children preferred A altogether and 44 preferred B **a**. So B was more popular **b**.

e **1/2 marks awarded. a** The student has given a verbal description of the data but has not interpreted them. To interpret data means to say what they indicate and involves going beyond what is in the table. **b** There is some interpretation in the very last sentence, 'So B was more popular'. This can be given 1 mark. 1 mark out of 2 is awarded.

(b) The result is not significant. This is because to be significant it has to be less than 5% and 7.27 is more than 5% **a**.

e **0 marks awarded. a** The student is confused here, comparing the obtained value of 7.27 with the minimum level of significance. No marks could therefore be awarded for comparing the obtained value with the stated value. This answer does not receive any credit.

(c) Standard deviations are a more sensitive calculation and account for variability around the mean. As a result of this they may be more reliable **a**.

e **0 marks awarded. a** The student has not answered the question. It is correct that standard deviations are sensitive and do account for variability around the mean, but the real issue of why they are used in addition to means has not been addressed. This answer does not receive any credit.

(d)(i) Parametric tests give a better calculation of statistical significance **a**.

e **0 marks awarded. a** This is an example of a vague answer. The answer must be more specific and clear, perhaps including a term such as 'power-efficient'. If you have difficulty conveying your answer in just one sentence, then elaborate with an example. For example, you could say, 'In testing for statistical significance between males and females in a visuo-spatial test, you are more likely to find a significant difference using a parametric test than if using a non-parametric test'. No marks are awarded here.

(ii) The data must be normally distributed **a**. The level of measurement must be interval **b**.

e **2/2 marks awarded. a** Strictly speaking the data should be drawn from a normally distributed population. However, in practice, examiners tend to be generous in their interpretation of an answer such as this. 1 mark can be given for the point about normal distribution and **b** another for the correct level of measurement.

(e) One variable could have been the mathematics test. It might have been easier **a**.

ⓔ 1/2 marks awarded. a This is a fair comment but gets only 1 mark, as an explanation for the identified variable (the easier mathematics test) is lacking. A possible explanation is that two more months of mathematics teaching meant that the children gained in competence and found the test easier. Therefore the scores would have been higher.

> **(f)** The children probably did not know that they were taking part in a study. Even though they are used to taking tests, this was not just about their progress but about the head wanting her school to be good at mathematics, manipulating the teaching and using their test scores for that purpose **b**. This is misleading, unethical and deceptive **a**.

ⓔ 2/2 marks awarded. a The student has selected a relevant issue, deception, and therefore gains 1 mark. **b** The issue is well explained. The student does point out that the teaching was manipulated and that testing, though a normal aspect of the school curriculum, did serve a purpose other than just the one intended, which is deception. A second mark was given for the explanation.

> **(g)** You could check the reliability of the test by repeating it to see if the same results can be replicated. This is called test-retest reliability **a** and if the results are similar **b**, then the test is reliable.

ⓔ 2/3 marks awarded. a The student has correctly identified test-retest reliability as one way of testing reliability and 1 mark can be given for describing this: that the test should be 'repeated'. **b** A second mark can be given for mentioning the expected outcome if the test is reliable, i.e. 'if the results are similar'. More could still be done with this answer, such as commenting on statistical analyses.

> **(h)** The category system would include disruptive and non-disruptive behaviour. This would be written down on a piece of paper divided in two, so that you would have a clear separation between the two categories **b**. I would observe the behaviour for 2–3 days in all the maths lessons and the other student would observe another 2–3 days. This would give about 5 hours, which is enough **c**. For reliability we could repeat the study **d**. For ethical considerations we would write a letter to all the parents for permission first **e a**.

ⓔ 1/5 marks awarded. a The student has benefited from the bullet-point list for structuring the answer. However, the actual content does not seem to show evidence of any practical experience of observational research. **b** The category system is unsatisfactory: it does not contain clearly defined examples of the target behaviour. **c** The sampling is ill considered — simply a division of labour but with no controls in place. **d** Reliability is inappropriately applied. **e** There is some merit in the letter to parents, for which 1 mark can be given.

Total for this question: 9 out of 20 marks — grade E.

Student B

(a) B was the preferred method for the boys and A was the preferred method for the girls **a**. Nearly three-quarters of the boys preferred B over A and 60% of the girls preferred A to B **b**. Overall though, most of the children preferred method B to method A **c**.

ⓔ **2/2 marks awarded. a** This student has gone straight into what is required, the interpretation of the data. 1 mark can be given for the comparison between boys and girls in the first sentence. **b** The student has also given percentage comparisons, which are correct but are not required. **c** The second mark can be given for the last sentence, where a comparison between the two methods is made. Notice that the student has addressed gender comparisons and teaching methods in general.

(b) The result is significant. This is because the obtained value of 7.27 is more than the stated table value of 3.841 **b** at the minimum 5% level of significance **c**. In fact, it is more than the stated table value of 6.635 at the 0.01 or 1% level of significance **a d**.

ⓔ **2/2 marks awarded. a** This is a straightforward, accurate and clear answer. **b** The student knows exactly which two values to compare and how to interpret the levels of significance and come to a conclusion. 1 mark is given for comparing the obtained value of 7.27 with the stated value of 3.841. **c** The second mark is given for stating that, 'The result is significant … at the minimum 5% level of significance'. **d** The comment about the 1% level confirms the student's understanding of the interpretation of critical values tables.

(c) Means just give an average summary score. However, although they represent every single score, they cannot give any information as to how spread out these scores are within the set, e.g. if they are all close to the mean or if there is a wide variation. Standard deviations can provide this information **a**.

ⓔ **1/1 mark awarded. a** The student has explained what information the mean is not able to provide but which the standard deviation can provide. This is all the question requires.

(d) (i) Parametric tests are more sensitive to the features of the data collected **a**, which means that unlike non-parametric tests, they do not rank data but use all the information available **b**.

ⓔ **1/1 mark awarded. a** 1 mark can be given for stating that parametric tests are more sensitive. **b** The elaboration is not actually required for the 1 mark, but it does serve to show that the student is well informed.

(ii) The variances of the two sets of scores should be similar (homogeneity of variance) **a**. However, the *t*-tests are robust so the data can depart from this assumption, particularly with related samples or unrelated samples with similar sized groups **b c**.

ⓔ **1/2 marks awarded. c** This is an informed and accurate answer. **a** It is good to see students using terminology, 'homogeneity of variance', which gains 1 mark. **b** However, the student has given only one criterion and seems to have forgotten about another.

(e) One possible variable, other than the teaching method itself which could account for the superior test scores following teaching method B, could be the practice effect **a**. Test B was the second test and it is possible that scores on this test were higher because they had already practised and got used to the test from the first time round. Therefore they would have done better **b**.

ⓔ **2/2 marks awarded. a** The variable identified is appropriate and so 1 mark is given for 'the practice effect'. **b** The explanation is concise, accurate and to the point, and worthy of a second mark.

(f) In any piece of research a participant has the right to withdraw **a**, but in this study the children are in school and cannot refuse to do tests. What the head must do is to bear this in mind when considering the situation the children are in and whether it is reasonable for them to continue. Is it not beyond what would normally have been expected **b**?

ⓔ **2/2 marks awarded. a** The issue selected is a difficult one, but the student has successfully explained it. 1 mark can be given for the issue, the right to withdraw, **b** and a second mark for the explanation of why and how it should still be considered. This is quite a subtle explanation and one that could quite easily have collapsed.

(g) The test has to be repeated **a**, usually after some period of time so that the teachers cannot remember what answer they gave the first time, although sometimes you can use different versions of the same test **b**. The two sets of scores should be compared for similarity. If the test is reliable then the scores will be very similar **c**. A test of correlation such as Spearman's rho can be carried out on the data.

A high positive significant correlation should be found if the test is reliable **d e**.

ⓔ **3/3 marks awarded. e** This answer contains all that is needed. **a** 1 mark can be given for the test being repeated. **b** The point about allowing for forgetting and different versions of the same test is good, but not essential to gain credit. **c** A second mark can be given for expected similarity of scores if the test is reliable. **d** A final mark can be given for the statistical analysis, which is correct. This is an excellent answer.

(h) Plan

- **Categories**. Types of disruptive behaviour to be checked out in a pilot study after discussion with another psychology student. Suggestions are: talking to others while teacher is teaching; talking to other students during work; getting up from the desk and distracting others; shouting out; engaging in anti-learning activities such as throwing paper across the classroom **b**.
- **Sampling**. One week of lessons split up into 10-minute intervals. Every 10 minutes, record behaviour taking place and enter ticks on tally sheet for type of disruptive behaviour, if any **c**.
- **Reliability**. Inter-observer reliability. Check the recordings for the behaviours I have made with those of the other psychology student. If these are similar then we have inter-observer reliability. Can do a correlation **d**.
- **Ethical considerations**. Consent: from the head who is *in loco parentis*. Fully inform the head of aims and structure of research. Do not cause any psychological harm during the actual research, e.g. do not make children feel uncomfortable, do not pass comment or judgement. Fully debrief head at the end of the study, keep all information confidential and preserve the anonymity of children **a e f**.

ⓔ **5/5 marks awarded. a** The student has responded to all the requirements and shown evidence of very sound knowledge and understanding of observational research. **b** The categories are realistic and target behaviours are identified. **c** The account of sampling — entering behaviours on a record sheet — suggests practical experience of carrying out an observation. **d** A check on inter-observer reliability is appropriate. **e** Finally, ethical issues are given detailed consideration including consent, protection from harm, debriefing, confidentiality and anonymity. **f** There is enough information here to allow the reader to implement the plan. The full 5 marks can be awarded: I mark each for categories, sampling and reliability, and 2 marks for ethics.

Total for this question: 19 out of 20 marks — grade A.

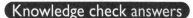

Knowledge check answers

1 The chemical substance produced by an endocrine gland is hormone.

2 Possible examples are: dilates pupils; increases rate of breathing; increases heart rate; increases action of adrenal glands; diverts blood from the stomach to the muscles; inhibits digestion; releases sugar.

3 Monozygotic twins are identical twins formed from the same fertilised egg and dizygotic twins are formed from two fertilised eggs. Dizygotic twins are genetically as similar as any pair of siblings, sharing about 50% of the same genes, whereas monozygotic twins have the same genes i.e. 100%.

4 An adaptive behaviour is one that promotes an individual's survival and reproduction and the potential survival of their genetic line.

5 The probability of the response being repeated in the future is increased.

6 The picture of the romantic meeting is the UCS as such a meeting naturally promotes the feeling of well-being, happiness and relaxation. These are all strong positive reactions. Alcohol is the conditioned stimulus as alcohol does not naturally promote such feelings but only through association with the picture of a romantic meeting.

7 Suggested answers: reinforcement; reinforcement of simpler behaviours; step-by step progression (to the desired behaviour); successive approximation.

8 Secondary reinforcement is a reinforcer that is not naturally reinforcing e.g. money but becomes a reinforcer because it is associated with a primary reinforcer e.g. food (something that is essential to survival).

9 In vicarious reinforcement or indirect reinforcement, learning is not the result of a learner's own personal and direct experience of reinforcement but a result of seeing someone else, the model, being reinforced. So the learner does not experience the reinforcement directly or personally but indirectly, through observing another person's experience.

10 Vicarious punishment.

11 Methods include: laboratory-based studies/experiments; computer programmes; computer models; scanning techniques; electrical recording. 'Case studies' is not an appropriate answer because, although they are used to investigate mental processes, they lack objectivity.

12 (i) We cannot see how some aspects of the nervous system, such as memory, are operating so we need a hypothetical representation or a 'mini theory' to help us describe and explain mental processes; (ii) a means of gaining information: a model can be tested by experimental or other means and in the light of research findings might be adapted or replaced.

13 Ego defence mechanisms have to be unconsciously motivated because their function is to protect the conscious mind from anxiety. If they were conscious then they would not be effective.

14 Fixation is an attachment to a particular stage of psychosexual development. The individual's libido becomes attached to that stage because of over- or under-gratification during that stage.

15 State of incongruence.

16 Deficiency needs or motives include: physiological needs; safety needs; love and belonging needs; self-esteem needs.

17 Darwin's theory of evolution was an important factor in Freud's emphasis on the sexual instinct. In Darwin's theory, survival of the individual and therefore the species is ensured through an innate and powerful reproductive drive. Furthermore, the view of humans as animals suggested to Freud that social behaviour is just a thin veneer covering barely controlled primitive urges and desires. This is reflected in Freud's psychodynamic theory.

18 Possible answers: the focus on internal mediating cognitive factors as opposed to behaviourist mechanical S-R focus; behaviour learned in social/interpersonal situations; role of cognitive factors in observational learning; specific interest in human learning especially the acquisition of social and moral behaviour.

19 Hypothalamus (increased aggression when overactive); amygdala (inhibits aggression). Limbic system is also an acceptable answer.

20 The behaviourist approach takes an extreme hard determinism position.

21 Concordance is the level of agreement between individuals or two sets of individuals for a given trait. The concordance rate is expressed as a percentage.

22 Extraneous variables are not controlled; IV is not manipulated; there is no random allocation of participants.

23 The behaviourist approach breaks down complex learning to simple components or S-R associations that have been learned.

24 Higher-level explanations are more holistic, such as explanations at the societal, political, sociological level. Such high-level explanations might consider the context in which a person lives. Lower-level explanations are more reductionist, such as explanations at the level of neurons.

25 Objective knowledge is knowledge based on facts: that which is physical, publicly verifiable and externally observable.

26 This is a criticism of Freud's psychodynamic theory. A limitation of the idiographic approach is that generalisations cannot reasonably be made to a wider population. Freud's case study method is clearly idiographic yet his theory of personality produced general laws of behaviour.

27 Likely answers: humanistic approach = free will vs. behaviourist approach = determinism; humanistic approach = subjective conscious experience vs. behaviourist approach = observable behaviour only needs to be studied; humanistic approach = each individual is unique vs. behaviourist approach = universal laws of learning.

28 Possible answers: laboratory experiments (number of words recalled); observations; recording of neuronal activity (in a particular part of the brain when undergoing a task); scans.

29 Possible answers: measures of central tendency; measures of dispersion; measures of correlation; graphs, bar charts; pie charts; frequency distributions.

30 A one-tailed hypothesis predicts an effect (i.e. a difference or a correlation) in one direction whereas a two-tailed hypothesis predicts two possible outcomes.

31 There is a 1% risk of a Type I error. The risk of this error is equivalent to the significance level being used.

32 Parametric tests are less likely to result in a Type II error. They are more powerful and not in need of as high a number of scores/participants as non-parametric tests to match their efficiency, so more likely to be able to correctly reject the null hypothesis.

33 Discrete data is measurement that is separate or distinct, falling into a category of its own e.g. either male or female. There are no gradations within, unlike continuous data such as height or time where there are gradations such as 1, 2, 3, or seconds.

34 Control: the experimenter's ability to manipulate the IV and control the effect of extraneous variables.

35 A time gap must be built in to allow for some forgetting of the responses given on the occasion of the first testing e.g. IQ test

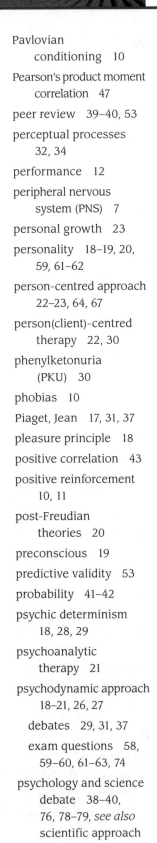

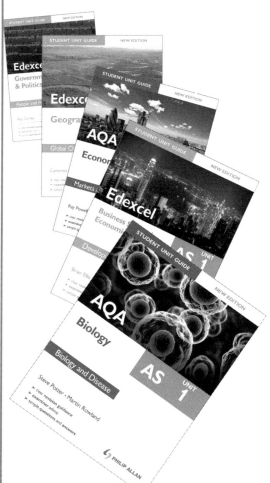

 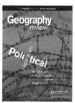  

Be an expert in all your 4 legal subjects